The Ultimate Ninja Dual Zone
Air Fryer Cookbook
for UK

The Easy, Energy-Saving & Tasty Recipes to Satisfy Your Family's Favorites Incl. Tips and Tricks |Full Color Pictures Version

John J. Bradshaw

Contents

INTRODUCTION

As a passionate home cook and foodie, I understand the significance of versatility, efficiency, and, especially, the incredible joy that comes from making homemade dishes for my family. I've been obsessed with air frying over the past few years. It seems to me like a perfect way to cook fried foods without lots of oil. This is a good and natural way to drop some pounds and stay healthy but not miss out on my favourite foods. A few years ago I needed a larger Air Fryer so I decided to purchase the Ninja Foodi MAX Dual Zone; it turned out great! Besides being practical daily, the Ninja Foodi is the perfect kitchen appliance for family gatherings thanks to its capacity.

The Ninja Foodi MAX Dual Zone is a unique kitchen appliance, designed to fry, bake and roast foods with minimal oil. It cooks my favourite foods in an easy and fast way, helping me to avoid that there's nothing-to-eat situation on the weeknights! So, I can prepare my fried foods just as I would in a regular frying pan. However, the Ninja Air Fryer revolutionized the way I eat and cook by utilizing cutting-edge technology. Lovely! I have taken the art of frying to the next level and decided to create this cookbook. In this cookbook, I've curated a selection of 120 recipes that showcase the incredible capabilities of the Ninja Foodi MAX Dual Zone. As a foodie who has embraced the wholesome principles of the Mediterranean diet, I will share with you a treasure trove of 120 Mediterranean recipes designed specifically for the Ninja Foodi. From light bites to succulent seafood dishes, and even luscious desserts, you will effortlessly bring restaurant-quality flavours of the Mediterranean cuisine to your dining table! I managed to combine the richness of Mediterranean flavours with the efficiency of air frying, creating wholesome and nutritious meals that celebrate the essence of the healthiest diet in the world! I love the vibrant dishes of the Mediterranean, that fusion of flavours, textures, and nutritional benefits! From fresh vegetables to nutritious seafood and aromatic herbs, the Mediterranean diet is a great inspiration to me!

So, let's put your Ninja Foodi into action! Let's explore the great potential that the Ninja Foodi

MAX Dual Zone unlocks for Mediterranean-inspired dishes, making every bite a celebration of incredible taste and vibrant good health!

3 Essential Things You Should Know About the Ninja Foodi MAX Dual Zone
1. The anatomy of the Ninja Foodi MAX Dual Zone. There are heating elements and specially designed fans that distribute the hot air evenly throughout the cooking chamber. Thanks to this cutting-edge hot air technology and air-tight, compact design, this incredible machine can cook your food evenly from all angles, producing that juicy, moist interior and golden-

brown, crunchy exterior!

Further, there are removable cooking drawers, as well as crisper plates. In fact, this magical device has two independent kitchen zones so you can cook two meals, both ready at the same time! The Ninja Foodi has a user-friendly display with all the necessary information. If you are a beginner, you can easily navigate through cooking functions, time and temperature controls. You can simply use the TEMP and TIME arrows to set the temperature and time to adjust the parameters according to the particular recipe.

2. Six different cooking functions.

You can choose from six different functions – AIR FRY, BAKE, ROAST, REHAT, DEHYDRATE, MAX CRISP. You can also select times and temperatures in each drawer to create complete meals – main courses and side dishes at the same time.

AIR FRY – Unlike the most popular frying techniques, Air Fryers use a small amount of oil but produce loads of flavour. Moreover, you do not need to preheat the pan – it can heat up quickly and distribute the heat evenly. It's all about the good technique!

BAKE – From the best savoury muffins to Italian pizza and Greek pastries, your Ninja Foodi can do it all! This is a pretty straightforward process. Place your food flat in the cooking basket or a baking tin; flip it halfway through the cooking time. Top it with cheese for savoury delights or honey for desserts, and you will enjoy delicious restaurant-style foods in no time!

ROAST – Roasting, grilling, and broiling are specific cooking techniques that use extremely high temperatures and direct heat to make a fine char on the top of your foods. And this is a cinch in your Ninja Foodi MAX Dual Zone! The "ROAST" function is perfect for skinless poultry, fish steaks, and melting toppings on traditional Mediterranean mousakas and casseroles. This is the most convenient way to create that perfectly charred surface on the top of your favourite food; plus, they turn out moist and succulent on all sides. Lovely!

REHEAT – Set your machine at around 160°C for up to 5 to 6 minutes. You cannot only revive leftovers but make them crisp and delicious again. You can also toast bread and pastries, making them as flavorful as freshly made!

DEHYDRATE – Imagine making Mediterranean-inspired dried figs and sun-dried tomatoes in the comfort of your kitchen! The Ninja Foodi MAX Dual Zone will help you to prepare your own dried fruits and vegs in the most convenient way! If you are eager to improve your diet with healthier and tastier alternatives to traditional delights, the "DEHYDRATE" button will be one of your favourites!

MAX CRISP – Quick and delicious dinners on busy weeknights will become your reality with this function! This is a perfect solution for smaller quantities of frozen food that cook at a high temperature. Plus, you do not need to thaw the frozen foods before you cook them on this function. Chicken dippers, nuggets, mozzarella sticks, potato pops, and onion rings will turn out perfect, just like from your favourite delivery service!

3. SYNC and MATCH

You can manually program each zone so they start and finish at the same time. If you cook foods with the same cooking time and temperature, place them in both zones. Now, simply select zone 1 and choose the function; then, select "MATCH" to duplicate settings across both zones. Press the "START/STOP" button. On the other hand, if you cook foods with different cooking times and temperatures, place them in both zones. Then, select the particular function for each zone and adjust the time and temperature; lastly, simply press the "SYNC" button and they will finish at the same time!

How to Clean the Ninja Foodi MAX Dual Zone
To keep your Ninja Foodi in perfect condition, first and foremost, read the manufacturer's instructions for any specific cleaning recommendations. Then, make a habit of cleaning it after each use to ensure safe and enjoyable cooking experiences. There are four basic steps:
1. Before starting, make sure the appliance is unplugged and completely cooled down. Discard any accumulated crumbs or debris.
2. Wipe down the interior of your machine using damp clothes or tea towels. This will remove potential stains or grease. Be sure not to get any liquid inside the electrical components. If there are any food particles on the heating element, gently remove them with a soft brush or cloth.
3. Take out all the removable accessories such as the cooking basket, crisper plates, and bakeware. Wash them in s warm soapy water using a non-abrasive sponge; a mild dishwashing liquid will do the best job! Rinse each part thoroughly and allow them to air dry before storing!
4. Now, clean the exterior of your appliance, including the control panel, with a slightly damp cloth.

Possible Risks of the Ninja Foodi MAX Dual Zone
Electrical hazards may occur with electrical devices. Ensure the machine is properly grounded and avoid using damaged parts. Unplug the appliance if you notice any electrical issues. Always

follow the manufacturer's guidelines.

Keep flammable materials away from the appliance and do not leave it unattended. It is essential to follow recommended cooking times and temperatures.

Be cautious of hot surfaces, especially the cooking zones. The appliance gets hot during operation, so make sure to use oven mitts and other protective gear.

With air frying, there is a risk of hot oil splattering. Keep a safe distance and avoid overfilling the cooking baskets.

Be especially cautious with sharp edges on components. Regularly inspect and maintain your Air Fryer. Replace malfunctioning and damaged components promptly. Regularly check the seals and gaskets for any signs of damage; replace if necessary.

Be mindful of allergens and clean the parts to prevent the transfer of foods that contain allergens.

There is a risk of overcooking or drying out food in the Ninja Foodi MAX Dual Zone as with any other Air Fryer. Be mindful of recommended cooking times and temperatures, and occasionally check and stir your food.

Tips and Tricks for the Ninja Foodi MAX Dual Zone

Explore your multi-cooker and be creative.

Take advantage of the machine's ability to air fry, bake, roast, and more. Experiment with different cooking techniques to create complex and flavourful dishes. Go ahead and use the accessories that come with the Ninja Foodi MAX Dual Zone.

Spice it up!

Season your ingredients before placing them in the cooking basket for better flavour infusion. This trick is essential for items like broccoli, potatoes and other "dull" vegetables.

Overfilling is a big no-no!

Do not overfill the cooking baskets with foods to avoid undercooking; also, avoid excess oil to prevent splattering. The ingredients always absorb as much oil as needed, so too much oil can only be counterproductive!

Keep an eye on the crisping process.

If you cook food with a higher fat content, adjust the cooking time and presets to prevent over-crisping and burning.

Use a meat thermometer.

This is especially recommended for larger cuts of meat. Undercooked meats are potentially harmful to your health. Harmful bacteria such as Escherichia coli and Salmonella in undercooked meat can cause foodborne illnesses. On the other hand, overcooked meat can become dry and tough. Different meats have different recommended internal temperatures for the best taste. The internal temperature can affect the quality and texture of meats, ensuring that meats are cooked to their optimal flavour and tenderness.

Shake, shake halfway through.

Shaking and flipping your foods will help ensure all sides are exposed to the hot air. Do not forget to flip the food halfway through the cooking time to achieve even cooking; unless otherwise specified.

Take advantage of the dual cooking zones.

Take the most out of your Ninja Foodi MAX Dual Zone and cook foods with varied cooking times simultaneously. You can cook a main course and a side dish at the same time and save your time and energy.

Follow the recipes.

Last but not least, follow cooking times and temperatures to create perfect air-fried foods, especially if you are a novice. Later, you can experiment with cooking times and temperatures to find the perfect settings according to your personal preferences.

10 Frequently Asked Questions

1. Do I need to preheat my Ninja Foodi MAX Dual Zone?

The answer is – yes and no! Preheating ensures that the air fryer reaches the desired temperature before cooking, leading to better results. However, if you forget to preheat your appliance, it will not drastically affect the final results!

2. How do I use the different cooking functions?

To understand the settings and functions available, including air frying, baking and any other features, read the manufacturer's guidelines and follow the recipes.

3. What safety features does the Ninja Foodi MAX Dual Zone have?

There are safety features such as auto-shutoff, overheat protection, and other safety measures that are integrated into the appliance.

4. Are there any recommended accessories for the Ninja Foodi MAX Dual Zone?

Yes, there are amazing accessories on the UK market that can enhance your cooking experience! They include grill pans, silicone pans, muffin cases, paper liners, and dehydrator racks.

5. Why is my Ninja Foodi MAX Dual Zone not cooking properly?

Distribute the items evenly in the cooking basket. Avoid overcrowding, as this can block air circulation. Leave some space for the air to circulate. Consider using a cooking spray to evenly coat the items. For larger items, consider pre-cooking (such as boiling and steaming) or partially cooking before air frying.

6. What is the capacity of each cooking zone?

The general capacity is 9.5 litres. For instance, the drawers can fit a whole chicken (around 2kg) or 1.4kg of chips.

7. Can I cook frozen food directly in the Ninja Foodi MAX Dual Zone?

Absolutely! There is a useful function – MAX CRISP, so you do not have to thaw and prepare your food in advance. This is a great option for meal prepping, too.

8. How do I prevent smoke?

Address common reasons for smoke, clean excess oil from the appliance, and maintain it regularly.

9. How do I prevent food from sticking to the cooking basket?

Always use a small amount of oil and take advantage of baking parchment and tin foil.

10. What can I cook in my Ninja Foodi MAX Dual Zone?

These items include common foods that can be cooked in every air fryer, such as fish, chips, vegetables, and baked goods. Plus, thanks to the DEHYDRATE and ROAST function, you can make dried fruits and vegetables, as well as casseroles and traybakes.

So, preheat your Ninja Foodi MAX Dual Zone, grab this cookbook, and let's dive into a magical world of air-fried Mediterranean delights!

CHAPTER 1
BREAKFAST

OATMEAL WITH DRIED BLUEBERRIES

Serves 5
Prep time: 6 hours
Cook time: 20 minutes

Per Serving:
Calories: 355
Fat: 7.5g
Carbs: 66.8g
Fiber: 12.2g
Protein: 13.1g

- 1 tsp coconut oil
- 1 tbsp chia seeds
- 150ml apple sauce
- 1 / 2 tsp almond extract
- 1 tsp ground cardamom
- 1 tsp ground cinnamon
- A pinch of sea salt
- A pinch of grated nutmeg
- 250g blueberries, fresh or frozen
- 300g porridge oats
- 300ml full-fat almond milk
- 150ml agave syrup

1. Brush the inside of a baking tin with coconut oil. Thoroughly combine all the ingredients, except blueberries. Spoon the mixture into the prepared baking tin.
2. Place blueberries on a baking tin lined with baking parchment. Spray them with cooking oil
3. Add the baking tin with oatmeal to the zone 1 drawer; add the blueberries to the zone 2 drawer.
4. Select zone 1 and pair it with "BAKE" at 180°C for 20 minutes. Select zone 2 and pair it with "DEHYDRATE" at 60°C for 6 hours. Select "SYNC" followed by the "START / STOP" button.
5. Divide the porridge between serving bowls; garnish each serving with dried blueberries. Devour!

HASH BROWNS WITH FETA CHEESE

Serves 6
Prep time: 10 minutes
Cook time: 33 minutes

Per Serving:
Calories: 343
Fat: 16.3g
Carbs: 33.7g
Fiber: 4.2g
Protein: 17.9g

- 800g waxy potato (such as Charlotte)
- 8 large eggs, whisked
- 200g onion, peeled and chopped
- 200g carrots, trimmed and grated
- A large handful of fresh parsley leaves, chopped
- 1 heaped tsp Aleppo pepper
- Sea salt and ground black pepper, to taste
- 1 tbsp olive oil
- 200g feta cheese, crumbled

1. Boil the potatoes for 15 minutes; drain. Peel the potatoes and coarsely grate them into a bowl.
2. Add the potatoes, along with the other ingredients, to the mixing bowl. Mix to combine well and spoon the mixture into two lightly oiled baking tins.
3. Lower the tins into the drawers. Select zone 1 and pair it with "BAKE" at 180°C for 18 minutes. Select "MATCH" followed by the "START / STOP" button.

Bon appétit!

FALL BUTTERNUT SQUASH MUFFINS

Serves 8
Prep time: 10 minutes
Cook time: 20 minutes

Per Serving:
Calories: 337
Fat: 10.7g
Carbs: 52.4g
Fiber: 4g
Protein: 9.1g

- 300g pumpkin puree, without salt
- 200 plain flour
- 180g old-fashioned rolled oats, plus extra for sprinkling
- 1 tsp bicarbonate of soda
- 1 tsp baking powder
- 150g golden syrup
- 2 large eggs, beaten
- 60ml coconut oil
- 130ml natural yoghurt
- 2 tsp pumpkin spice mix

1. Very lightly butter 8 muffin cases.
2. In a bowl, thoroughly combine all the dry ingredients. In a separate bowl, whisk the liquid ingredients.
3. Slowly and gradually, add the liquid mixture to the dry ingredients. Spoon the batter into the prepared muffin cases. Place the muffin cases in both drawers.
4. Select zone 1 and pair it with "BAKE" at 170°C for 20 minutes. Select "MATCH" followed by the "START / STOP" button.
5. Let your muffins cool on a rack for about 10 minutes before serving. Enjoy!

COURGETTE FRITTERS

Serves 6
Prep time: 10 minutes
Cook time: 20 minutes

Per Serving:
Calories: 318
Fat: 12.6g
Carbs: 33.4g
Fiber: 2.2g
Protein: 18g

- 600g courgette, coarsely grated
- 2 large eggs, beaten
- 200g plain flour
- 1 tsp baking powder
- 1 tsp bicarbonate of soda
- 1 medium onion, sliced
- 1 tbsp olive oil
- 1 tsp dried oregano
- 1 tsp dried basil
- 1 tbsp fresh parsley leaves, chopped
- Sea salt and black pepper to taste
- 180g parmesan cheese, grated

1. In a mixing bowl, coarsely grate the courgette and then, wring out the liquid with a clean tea towel.
2. Add the other ingredients to the bowl. Line the bottom of the crisper plates with baking parchment.
3. Shape the mixture into patties, flattening them down with the back of a spoon into disc shapes.
4. Place the patties on crisper plates. Select zone 1 and pair it with "AIR FRY" at 180°C for 20 minutes. Select "MATCH" followed by the "START / STOP" button.
5. When zone 1 time reaches 10 minutes, turn them over, and cook for a further 10 minutes, until thoroughly cooked.

Bon appétit!

BURRITO EGG WRAPS

Serves 4
Prep time: 10 minutes
Cook time: 10 minutes

Per Serving:
Calories: 334
Fat: 19.6g
Carbs: 30.7g
Fiber: 6g
Protein: 11.2g

- 1 tsp olive oil
- 4 eggs
- 4 whole-meal tortilla wraps
- 1 medium avocado, stoned, peeled, and sliced
- 100g baby spinach
- 1 small Persian cucumber, sliced
- 100g Kalamata olives, sliced
- 1 medium ripe tomato, sliced

1. Spray tartlet moulds with olive oil. Then, crack an egg in each tartlet mould. Add the eggs to the zone 1 drawer and the tortillas to the zone 2 drawer.
2. Select zone 1 and pair it with "BAKE" at 190°C for 10 minutes. Select zone 2 and pair it with "REHEAT" at 160°C for 3 minutes. Select "SYNC" followed by the "START / STOP" button.
3. To assemble your burritos: divide fried eggs, avocado slices, spinach, cucumber, olives, and tomato between tortilla wraps; wrap them up and serve immediately.
Enjoy!

ITALIAN BISCOTTI

Serves 8
Prep time: 15 minutes
Cook time: 35 minutes

Per Serving:
Calories: 204
Fat: 2.4g
Carbs: 37g
Fiber: 1.6g
Protein: 4.5g

- 300g plain flour
- 150g caster sugar
- 1 tsp baking powder
- 1 / 2 tsp bicarbonate of soda
- 4 tbsp hot water
- 100g olive oil
- 2 large eggs
- 1 tsp vanilla extract
- 1 tsp ground cinnamon
- A pinch of flaky sea salt

1. In a mixing bowl, thoroughly combine dry ingredients; in a separate bowl, whisk the liquid ingredients.
2. Gradually mix the liquid mixture ingredients into the dry ingredients; mix until it comes together into a dough.
3. You can add another 1 to 2 tablespoons of water if it's too difficult to knead the dough. Shape the mixture into two logs and lower them onto two lightly greased baking trays.
4. Lower the baking trays into the cooking basket.
5. Bake the logs at 180 degrees C for about 20 minutes; leave to cool for 15 minutes.
6. After that, cut the logs into 1-2cm-thick slices crosswise using a sharp knife. Return the biscotti to the baking tray and bake for a further 15 minutes.

SPICY OMELETTE CASSEROLE

Serves 8
Prep time: 5 minutes
Cook time: 15 minutes

Per Serving:
Calories: 199
Fat: 15.5g
Carbs: 4.7g
Fiber: 1.1g
Protein: 8.8g

- 10 medium eggs, beaten
- 5 tbsp cream cheese
- 3 spring onions, sliced
- 1 large tomato, diced
- 1 chilli pepper, chopped (e.g. Aleppo chilli pepper)
- 5 tbsp double cream
- 2 tbsp olive oil
- 2 tbsp anchovy paste

1. Remove a crisper plate from your Ninja Dual Zone Air Fryer.
2. In a bowl, whisk the eggs, double cream, and cheese until frothy. Fold in the other ingredients and whisk until everything is well incorporated.
3. Spoon the mixture into two lightly oiled baking trays. Add the baking trays to the cooking basket.
4. Select zone 1 and pair it with "BAKE" at 180°C for 15 minutes. Select "MATCH" followed by the "START / STOP" button.
5. When zone 1 time reaches 8 minutes, turn them over, and cook for a further 7 minutes or until thoroughly cooked.
6. Cut your omelettes into wedges and serve immediately.

Bon appétit!

COUSCOUS WITH VEGETABLES

Serves 4
Prep time: 5 minutes
Cook time: 24 minutes

Per Serving:
Calories: 254
Fat: 4.1g
Carbs: 45.2g
Fiber: 4.1g
Protein: 9.2g

- 1 medium courgette, quartered
- 2 medium bell pepper
- 200g Italian mushrooms, sliced
- 1 tbsp olive oil
- 1 tbsp Italian herbs
- Sea salt and ground black pepper, to taste
- 200g couscous
- 200ml water

1. Toss your vegetables with olive oil and spices; lower the courgette and mushrooms into the zone 1 drawer and peppers into the zone 2 drawer.
2. Select zone 1 and pair it with "AIR FRY" at 190°C for 16 minutes. Select zone 2 and pair it with "AIR FRY" at 200°C for 10 minutes. Select "SYNC" followed by the "START / STOP" button. Your vegetables will still be a bit crispy.
3. Meanwhile, cook your couscous in boiling water for about 10 minutes. Add your couscous to a lightly oiled casserole dish.
4. Add the other ingredients and gently stir to combine. Next, bake this delicious breakfast casserole at 190°C for about 8 minutes using the "BAKE" function. Enjoy!

AVOCADO AND CHERRY TOMATOES ON TOAST

Serves 4
Prep time: 5 minutes
Cook time: 15 minutes

Per Serving:
Calories: 174
Fat: 11.5g
Carbs: 16.5g
Fiber: 4.4g
Protein: 3.3g

- 100g cherry tomatoes
- 1 tbsp olive oil
- Sea salt and ground black pepper, to taste
- 4 regular slices of Italian bread
- 1 large avocado, stoned and mashed
- 1 tsp garlic granules

1. Toss cherry tomatoes with olive oil, salt, and black pepper to taste. Add cherry tomatoes to the Zone 1 drawer and the bread slices to the Zone drawer.
2. Select zone 1 and pair it with "AIR FRY" at 180°C for 15 minutes. Select zone 2 and pair it with "BAKE" at 185°C for 3 minutes. Select "SYNC" followed by the "START / STOP" button.
3. Put a slice of toasted bread on each plate and pile some avocado on top. Then sprinkle with the garlic granules, salt and pepper.
4. Arrange some cherry tomatoes on top.

Bon appétit!

POTATO ROSTI

Serves 8
Prep time: 10 minutes
Cook time: 12 minutes

Per Serving:
Calories: 210
Fat: 9.8g
Carbs: 24.4g
Fiber: 3.2g
Protein: 6.1g

- 800g Maris Piper potatoes, peeled and coarsely grated
- 4 large eggs, beaten
- 8 tbsp plain flour
- 1 tsp baking powder
- 2 green onions, sliced
- 1 tbsp olive oil
- 200g black olives, stoned and sliced
- 1 tbsp Mediterranean herb mix

1. Coarsely grate your potatoes; wring out the liquid with a clean tea towel.
2. Add the other ingredients to the grated potatoes. Line the bottom of the cooking basket with baking parchment.
3. Shape the mixture into patties, flattening them down with the back of a spoon into disc shapes. Add the patties to both drawers.
4. Select zone 1 and pair it with "BAKE" at 190°C for 12 minutes. Select "MATCH" followed by the "START / STOP" button.
5. When zone 1 time reaches 6 minutes, turn them over, and cook for a further 6 minutes or until thoroughly cooked.

Bon appétit!

GREEK PITA TOSTADAS

Serves 4
Prep time: 10 minutes
Cook time: 20 minutes

Per Serving:
Calories: 325
Fat: 10.8g
Carbs: 46.2g
Fiber: 6.6g
Protein: 14.1g

- 4 eggs
- 2 tsp olive oil
- 1 bell pepper, seeded and diced chopped
- 1 teaspoon oregano
- Sea salt and ground black pepper, to season
- 4 Greek pitas
- 4 tbsp sour cream
- 1 small courgette, diced
- 1 small red onion, finely
- 1 / 2 teaspoon rosemary
- 1 small tomato, diced
- 4 tbsp hummus

1. In a mixing bowl, whisk the eggs with sour cream, salt, and pepper. Spoon the mixture into muffin cases. Add them to the zone 1 drawer.
2. Toss the courgette and pepper with olive oil, salt, and black pepper; add them to the zone 2 drawer.
3. Select zone 1 and pair it with "AIR FRY" at 190°C for 15 minutes. Select zone 2 and pair it with "ROAST" at 200°C for 7 minutes. Select "SYNC" followed by the "START / STOP" button.
4. Top your pitas with all the ingredients and wrap them up!
5. Bake your tostadas in the preheated Air Fryer at 180 degrees C for about 5 minutes using the "REHEAT" function.

BREAKFAST COURGETTE ROSTI WITH PARMESAN CHEESE

Serves 5
Prep time: 10 minutes
Cook time: 12 minutes

Per Serving:
Calories: 481
Fat: 29.6g
Carbs: 23.4g
Fiber: 1.2g
Protein: 29.1g

- 400g courgette, coarsely grated
- 2 large eggs, beaten
- 50g plain flour
- 50g Parmesan cheese, grated
- 1 tsp baking powder
- 1 shallot, sliced
- 1 tbsp olive oil
- 1 tsp dried basil
- 1 tbsp fresh parsley leaves, chopped

1. In a mixing bowl, coarsely grate the courgette and then, wring out the liquid with a clean tea towel.
2. Add the other ingredients to the bowl. Line the bottom of the cooking basket with baking parchment.
3. Shape the mixture into patties, flattening them down with the back of a spoon into disc shapes.
4. Select zone 1 and pair it with "BAKE" at 190°C for 12 minutes. Select "MATCH" followed by the "START / STOP" button.
5. When zone 1 time reaches 6 minutes, turn them over, and cook for a further 6 minutes or until thoroughly cooked.

Bon appétit!

FRITTATA WITH GREENS

Serves 4
Prep time: 10 minutes
Cook time: 15 minutes

Per Serving:
Calories: 188
Fat: 13.8g
Carbs: 5g
Fiber: 1.6g
Protein: 10.2g

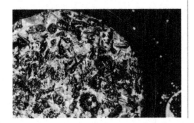

- 6 medium eggs, beaten
- 4 tbsp Greek yogurt
- 2 tbsp olive oil
- 2 green onions, chopped
- 100g Swiss chard, torn into pieces
- 100g baby spinach

1. In a bowl, whisk the eggs until frothy. Fold in the other ingredients and whisk until everything is well incorporated.
2. Spoon the mixture into two lightly oiled baking trays.
3. Select zone 1 and pair it with "BAKE" at 180°C for 15 minutes. Select "MATCH" followed by the "START / STOP" button.
4. When zone 1 time reaches 8 minutes, turn them over, and cook for a further 7 minutes or until thoroughly cooked.
5. Cut your frittata into pieces and serve immediately.
Bon appétit!

BREAKFAST COUSCOUS PORRIDGE WITH FIGS

Serves 4
Prep time: 10 minutes
Cook time: 15 minutes

Per Serving:
Calories: 260
Fat: 0.6g
Carbs: 57.2g
Fiber: 4.1g
Protein: 6.8g

- 200g couscous
- 200ml water
- 200g figs, halved
- 2 tbsp honey
- 1 tsp ground cumin

1. Cook your couscous in boiling water for about 10 minutes. Add your couscous followed by the water, honey and cumin to a lightly oiled baking tin.
2. Lower the baking tin into the zone 1 drawer and figs into the zone 2 drawer (with a crisper plate).
3. Select zone 1 and pair it with "BAKE" at 190°C for 15 minutes. Select zone 2 and pair it with "AI RFRY" at 200°C for 10 minutes. Select "SYNC" followed by the "START / STOP" button.
4. Top your couscous with frier figs and enjoy!

Serves 4
Prep time: 10 minutes
Cook time: 10 minutes

Per Serving:
Calories: 267
Fat: 16.5g
Carbs: 20.8g
Fiber: 4.4g
Protein: 10.3g

- 4 large eggs
- 1 tbsp olive oil
- 1 tsp dried dill weed
- 1 tsp dried parsley flakes
- Sea salt and ground black pepper, to taste
- 4 regular slices of Italian bread
- 1 large avocado, stoned and mashed

1. In a mixing bowl, whisk the eggs until pale and frothy. Now, add spices and spoon the egg mixture into a lightly greased baking tray.
2. Now, oil the bread slices with the olive oil.
3. Add the baking tray to the zone 1 drawer and the bread slices to the zone 2 drawer.
4. Select zone 1 and pair it with "BAKE" at 190°C for 10 minutes. Select zone 2 and pair it with "REHEAT" at 160°C for 3 minutes. Select "SYNC" followed by the "START / STOP" button
5. Serve scrambled eggs and avocado on toast and enjoy!

CHAPTER 2
SALADS

CRUNCHY HALLOUMI SALAD

Serves 8
Prep time: 10 minutes
Cook time: 6 minutes

Per Serving:
Calories: 416
Fat: 22.2g
Carbs: 35g
Fiber: 2.2g
Protein: 18.7g

- 2400g halloumi
- 2 medium eggs
- 1 tbsp Mediterranean spice mix
- 200g Romaine lettuce, torn into pieces
- 1 medium red onion, sliced
- 1 medium cucumber, sliced
- 2 tbsp fresh lemon juice
- 2 tbsp extra-virgin olive oil
- 120g plain flour
- 160g crushed cornflakes
- 1 tbsp olive oil

1. Cut the halloumi into fat chips. Now, set up your breading station. Place the flour in a shallow dish. In a separate dish, whisk the egg. Lastly, thoroughly combine the crushed cornflakes with spice mix in a third dish.
2. Start by dredging halloumi pieces in the flour; then, dip them into the egg. Press halloumi pieces into the cornflake mixture. Brush breaded halloumi pieces with olive oil.
3. Add the halloumi chips to both drawers.
4. Select zone 1 and pair it with "AIR FRY" at 190°C for 6 minutes. Select "MATCH" followed by the "START / STOP" button.
5. In the meantime, toss the other ingredients in a salad bowl.
6. Top your salad with halloumi chips and serve immediately. Bon appétit!

ASPARAGUS AND RICOTTA SALAD

Serves 6
Prep time: 10 minutes
Cook time: 10 minutes

Per Serving:
Calories: 156
Fat: 10.1g
Carbs: 10.5g
Fiber: 3g
Protein: 5.7g

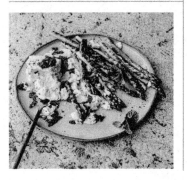

- 600g asparagus, cleaned and trimmed
- 2 tbsp extra-virgin olive oil
- Flaky sea salt and ground black pepper, to taste
- 1 tsp red pepper flakes, crushed
- 1 large bell pepper, deseeded and halved
- 1 large tomato, sliced
- 1 large red onion, sliced
- 160g ricotta salata, crumbled

1. Toss your asparagus and peppers with 1 tablespoon of olive oil and spices; toss until they are well coated on all sides.
2. Add the asparagus spears to the zone 1 drawer and peppers to the zone 2 drawer.
3. Select zone 1 and pair it with "ROAST" at 200°C for 10 minutes. Select "MATCH" followed by the "START / STOP" button.
4. When zone 1 time reaches 5 minutes, turn the vegetables over to ensure even cooking.
5. Cut the peppers into strips. Toss the roasted asparagus and peppers with the other ingredients; toss to combine well.
6. Top your salad with ricotta salata. Bon appétit!

COD SALAD WITH PEPPERS

Serves 4
Prep time: 10 minutes
Cook time: 15 minutes

Per Serving:
Calories: 406
Fat: 15.5g
Carbs: 39.4g
Fiber: 16.3g
Protein: 33.5g

- 600g cod fillets
- 4 bell peppers, whole
- 2 tbsp olive oil
- Flaky sea salt and ground black pepper, to taste
- 1 tsp Aleppo pepper
- 1 tsp dried rosemary
- 2 hearts of romaine lettuce, torn into pieces
- 1 large red onion, sliced
- Juice of 1 large lemon
- 3 tbsp extra-virgin olive oil

1. Coat cod fillets and peppers with olive oil and spices; rub them with the spice mixture on all sides.
2. Lower the fish into the zone 1 drawer and peppers into the zone 2 drawer.
3. Select zone 1 and pair it with "AIR FRY" at 200°C for 10 minutes. Select zone 2 and pair it with "ROAST" at 200°C for 15 minutes. Select "SYNC" followed by the "START / STOP" button.
4. Slice the fish and peppers into strips.
5. Toss lettuce and onion with lemon juice and extra-virgin olive oil. Top them with the roasted peppers and fish. Devour!

FATTOUSH SALAD

Serves 4
Prep time: 10 minutes
Cook time: 15 minutes

Per Serving:
Calories: 232
Fat: 8.4g
Carbs: 36.5g
Fiber: 5.5g
Protein: 6g

- 2 large pita bread, cut into triangles
- 1 large bell pepper, deseeded and sliced
- 2 tbsp extra-virgin olive oil
- Sea salt and ground black pepper, to taste
- 1 tsp red pepper flakes, crushed
- 1 head of lettuce, torn into pieces
- 1 small Persian cucumber, sliced
- 2 Roma tomatoes, diced
- 2 tbsp parsley leaves, chopped
- 1 tsp pomegranate molasses
- 1 tsp sumac
- 100g radishes, sliced

1. Toss pita bread and bell pepper with 1 tablespoon of olive oil, salt, and black pepper.
2. Lower the bread into the zone 1 drawer and peppers into the zone 2 drawer.
3. Select zone 1 and pair it with "BAKE" at 170°C for 5 minutes. Select zone 2 and pair it with "ROAST" at 200°C for 15 minutes. Select "SYNC" followed by the "START / STOP" button.
4. Slice the peppers into strips and reserve.
5. In a salad bowl, toss the remaining ingredients; top your salad with baked pita bread triangles and peppers.
Bon appétit!

MUSTARD POTATO SALAD

Serves 8
Prep time: 10 minutes
Cook time: 20 minutes

Per Serving:
Calories: 162
Fat: 7.6g
Carbs: 22.3g
Fiber: 3.2g
Protein: 2.8g

- 600g potatoes, peeled and diced (red or white potatoes)
- 4 tbsp extra-virgin olive oil
- Sea salt and ground black pepper, to taste
- 1 tsp dried rosemary
- 1 large red onion, sliced
- 1 sprig of fresh dill, chopped
- 1 tbsp white wine vinegar
- 1 tbsp Dijon mustard

1. Toss potatoes with 1 tablespoon of olive oil, salt, and black pepper; toss until they are well coated on all sides.
2. Add the potatoes to both drawers.
3. Select zone 1 and pair it with "AIR FRY" at 190°C for 20 minutes. Select "MATCH" followed by the "START / STOP" button.
4. When the potatoes are cool enough to handle, add them to a salad bowl.
5. Add the other ingredients to the bowl and gently stir to combine. Devour!

EPIC EGG SALAD

Serves 4
Prep time: 15 minutes
Cook time: 15 minutes

Per Serving:
Calories: 251
Fat: 16g
Carbs: 5.6g
Fiber: 0.8g
Protein: 13.6g

- 6 medium eggs, at room temperature
- 2 tbsp extra-virgin olive oil
- Sea salt and ground black pepper, to taste
- 2 fat garlic cloves, minced
- 1 small head of lettuce, torn into pieces
- 120g feta, crumbled
- 1 tsp Aleppo pepper
- 1 tbsp apple cider vinegar
- 1 tbsp fresh lemon juice

1. Lower the into the drawers.
2. Select zone 1 and pair it with "AIR FRY" at 130°C for 15 minutes. Select "MATCH" followed by the "START / STOP" button.
3. Transfer the eggs to an ice-cold water bath to stop cooking. Peel the eggs under cold running water and cut them into small pieces.
4. Toss the remaining ingredients in a salad bowl; add the hard-boiled eggs and gently stir to combine. Enjoy!

PARM AUBERGINE SALAD

Serves 8
Prep time: 10 minutes
Cook time: 12 minutes

Per Serving:
Calories: 381
Fat: 23.2g
Carbs: 14.5g
Fiber: 4.7g
Protein: 27g

- 1kgg aubergine, diced
- 4 tbsp extra-virgin olive oil
- Sea salt and ground black pepper, to taste
- 1 / 2 tsp za'atar
- 1 tsp Aleppo pepper
- 200g arugula
- 200g radishes, sliced
- 1 large cucumber, sliced
- 1 large lemon, juiced
- 2 tbsp fresh mint, chopped
- 200g parmesan cheese, preferably freshly grated

1. Toss aubergine pieces with 1 tablespoon of olive oil and spices. Lower them into both drawers.
2. Select zone 1 and pair it with "AIR FRY" at 200°C for 12 minutes. Select "MATCH" followed by the "START / STOP" button.
3. Toss your aubergine with the other vegetables; drizzle your salad with the lemon juice and the remaining olive oil; toss to combine well.
4. Serve garnished with freshly grated parmesan and mint.

Bon appétit!

ZESTY TUNA AND BROCCOLI SALAD

Serves 6
Prep time: 10 minutes
Cook time: 13 minutes

Per Serving:
Calories: 425
Fat: 12.4g
Carbs: 43.7g
Fiber: 16g
Protein: 41.5g

- 800g tuna fillets
- 2 tbsp olive oil
- 800g broccoli florets
- Flaky sea salt and ground black pepper, to taste
- 1 tsp Aleppo pepper
- 2 spring onions, sliced
- Juice of 1 large lemon
- 2 tbsp extra-virgin olive oil
- 2 celery stalks, chopped
- 1 large Greek cucumber, chopped
- 12 radishes, stems removed, chopped
- 12 fresh mint leaves, stems removed and chopped
- 1 tbsp good quality Dijon mustard

1. Coat tuna fillets and broccoli with 2 tablespoons of olive oil and spices; rub them with the spice mixture on all sides.
2. Lower the fish into the zone 1 drawer and the broccoli into the zone 2 drawer.
3. Select zone 1 and pair it with "AIR FRY" at 195°C for 13 minutes. Select zone 2 and pair it with "ROAST" at 200°C for 11 minutes. Select "SYNC" followed by the "START / STOP" button.
4. When zone 1 time reaches 7 minutes, turn the fish fillets over to promote even cooking; then, reinsert the drawer to resume cooking.
5. Slice the fish into strips.
6. Toss the remaining ingredients in a bowl. Top them with fish. Devour!

GRILLED COURGETTE SALAD

Serves 6
Prep time: 10 minutes
Cook time: 10 minutes

Per Serving:
Calories: 120
Fat: 8.2g
Carbs: 6.8g
Fiber: 1.4g
Protein: 5.5g

- 800g zucchini (courgette), sliced
- 4 tbsp extra-virgin olive oil
- Flaky sea salt and ground black pepper, to taste
- 1 tsp Aleppo pepper
- 1 tsp dried oregano
- 1 tsp dried rosemary
- 200g cherry tomatoes
- 1 bell pepper, deseeded and halved
- 1 small red onion, sliced
- 200g goat cheese, grated

1. Toss courgette with 1 tablespoon of olive oil and spices; toss until they are well coated on all sides.
2. Place the courgette slices in both drawers. Select zone 1 and pair it with "ROAST" at 200°C for 10 minutes. Select "MATCH" followed by the "START / STOP" button.
3. Toss roasted courgette with the other ingredients.
Devour!

ROASTED ALMONDS, FIG & GOAT CHEESE SALAD

Serves 6
Prep time: 10 minutes
Cook time: 10 minutes

Per Serving:
Calories: 480
Fat: 32.2g
Carbs: 33g
Fiber: 9.1g
Protein: 22.5g

- 200g almonds
- 10 figs, halved
- 400g mixed salad greens
- 2 tbsp extra-virgin olive oil
- 2 tbsp balsamic vinegar
- 250g goat cheese, crumbled
- 1 tbsp honey
- Sea salt and ground black pepper, to taste

1. Add the almonds to the zone 1 drawer and figs to the zone 2 drawer.
2. Select zone 1 and pair it with "AIR FRY" at 180°C for 7 minutes. Select zone 2 and pair it with "ROAST" at 200°C for 10 minutes. Select "SYNC" followed by the "START / STOP" button.
3. When zone 1 time reaches 4 minutes, stir the almonds to promote even cooking; then, reinsert the drawer to resume cooking.
4. When zone 2 time reaches 5 minutes, turn the figs over and reinsert the drawer to resume cooking.
5. In a salad bowl, toss all the ingredients. Top the salad with slivered almonds.
Devour!

SPICY CAULIFLOWER SALAD

Serves 6
Prep time: 10 minutes
Cook time: 13 minutes

Per Serving:
Calories: 305
Fat: 19.8g
Carbs: 17.3g
Fiber: 4.1g
Protein: 17.2g

- 800g cauliflower florets
- 200g cherry tomatoes, whole
- 2 tbsp harissa paste
- 1 tsp extra-virgin olive oil
- 1 tbsp honey
- 2 tbsp tahini (sesame paste)
- 2 tbsp soy sauce
- 2 tbsp white vinegar
- Sea salt and ground black pepper, to taste
- 240g goat cheese, crumbled

1. Toss cauliflower florets and bell peppers with harissa paste, olive oil, salt, and black pepper to taste. Add the cauliflower florets to the zone 1 drawer and tomatoes to the zone 2 drawer.
2. Select zone 1 and pair it with "AIR FRY" at 200°C for 13 minutes. Select zone 2 and pair it with "ROAST" at 200°C for 10 minutes. Select "SYNC" followed by the "START / STOP" button.
3. In a salad bowl, gently stir the cauliflower with tomatoes. Whisk the honey, tahini, soy sauce, vinegar, salt, and pepper for the dressing.
4. Dress your salad, top with goat cheese, and enjoy!

MEDITERRANEAN POULTRY SALAD

Serves 6
Prep time: 10 minutes
Cook time: 20 minutes

Per Serving:
Calories: 325
Fat: 18g
Carbs: 13.4g
Fiber: 3.5g
Protein: 30.2g

- 800g chicken breasts
- 2 tbsp extra-virgin olive oil
- Sea salt and ground black pepper, to taste
- 1 large red onion
- 1 small Persian cucumber, sliced
- 1 medium head of red cabbages, shredded
- 1 tbsp red wine vinegar

1. Toss the chicken and onion with 1 tablespoon of olive oil, salt, and black pepper to taste. Place the chicken in the zone 1 drawer and the onion in the zone 2 drawer.
2. Select zone 1 and pair it with "AIR FRY" at 200°C for 20 minutes. Select zone 2 and pair it with "ROAST" at 180°C for 10 minutes. Select "SYNC" followed by the "START / STOP" button.
3. In a salad bowl, gently stir the chicken with vegetables. Whisk the remaining 1 tablespoon of extra-virgin olive oil, vinegar, salt, and black pepper for the dressing.
4. Dress your salad and enjoy!

SALMON SALAD WITH MUSTARD DRESSING

Serves 6
Prep time: 10 minutes
Cook time: 14 minutes

Per Serving:
Calories: 351
Fat: 20.2g
Carbs: 13.4g
Fiber: 5.3g
Protein: 30.1g

- 800g salmon steak
- 2 tbsp olive oil
- Flaky sea salt and ground black pepper, to taste
- 1 large head of romaine lettuce, torn into pieces
- 1 large red onion, sliced
- 4 tbsp Kalamata olives, stoned and halved
- Juice of 1 large lemon
- 1 tbsp Dijon mustard
- 1 tbsp maple syrup
- 4 tbsp extra-virgin olive oil

1. Coat salmon steaks with olive oil, salt, and pepper on all sides.
2. Place the fish in both drawers. Select zone 1 and pair it with "ROAST" at 200°C for 14 minutes. Select "MATCH" followed by the "START / STOP" button.
3. Cook until the flesh is opaque and slice the salmon into bite-sized strips.
4. Meanwhile, whisk the lemon juice, mustard, maple syrup, and extra-virgin olive oil to create the dressing.
5. Divide the lettuce, onion, and olives between six plates, top with the fish, and then drizzle over the prepared dressing.

ROASTED GARLIC AUBERGINE SALAD

Serves 8
Prep time: 10 minutes
Cook time: 10 minutes

Per Serving:
Calories: 148
Fat: 7.7g
Carbs: 17.1g
Fiber: 7.4g
Protein: 3.7g

- 1kg aubergine, diced
- 4 tbsp extra-virgin olive oil
- 1 large garlic head, minced
- Sea salt and ground black pepper, to taste
- 1 tsp Aleppo pepper
- 2 head of romaine lettuce
- 2 medium cucumber, sliced
- 1 large lemon, juiced

1. Toss aubergine with 1 tablespoon of olive oil and spices. Wrap your garlic in a tin foil.
2. Lower the aubergine into the zone 1 drawer and the garlic head into the zone 2 drawer.
3. Select zone 1 and pair it with "AIR FRY" at 190°C for 10 minutes. Select zone 2 and pair it with "ROAST" at 185°C for 9 minutes. Select "SYNC" followed by the "START / STOP" button.
4. Toss your aubergine with the other vegetables. Leave the garlic to cool for a few minutes before squeezing it out of the shell.
5. Mash the garlic with the remaining olive oil until it forms a paste. Add the garlic paste to the salad and drizzle everything with the fresh lemon juice.

Bon appétit!

HARISSA FISH AND COUSCOUS SALAD

Serves 8
Prep time: 10 minutes
Cook time: 10 minutes

Per Serving:
Calories: 269
Fat: 11.2g
Carbs: 21.4g
Fiber: 4.9g
Protein: 20.1g

- 800g haddock fillets
- 1 tbsp olive oil
- 1 tsp cayenne pepper
- Sea salt and ground black pepper, to taste
- 2 tbsp rose harissa
- 400g cooked couscous
- 1 head romaine lettuce, torn into pieces
- 1 large red onion, sliced
- 1 large cucumber, sliced
- 4 tbsp Kalamata olives, stoned and halved
- 1 lemon, juiced
- 4 tbsp extra-virgin olive oil

1. Coat haddock fillets with olive oil, cayenne pepper, salt, and black pepper on all sides.
2. Lower the fish into both drawers.
3. Select zone 1 and pair it with "ROAST" at 200°C for 10 minutes. Select "MATCH" followed by the "START / STOP" button.
4. When zone 1 time reaches 5 minutes, turn haddock fillets over and top them with harissa paste; continue to cook for another 5 to 6 minutes, or until the flesh is opaque.
5. Slice the fish into bite-sized pieces.
6. Divide the couscous, lettuce, onion, cucumber, and olives between four serving bowls; top each salad with the fish, and then drizzle over the lemon juice and extra-virgin olive oil.
7. Serve with extra lemon wedges for squeezing over and enjoy!

CHAPTER 3
FISH & SEAFOOD

GRILLED SQUID RINGS

Serves 4
Prep time: 10 minutes
Cook time: 10 minutes

Per Serving:
Calories: 219
Fat: 8.9g
Carbs: 8.4g
Fiber: 4.9g
Protein: 0.6g

- 600g squid tubes, sliced into rings
- 2 tbsp olive oil
- 2 tbsp red cooking wine
- 2 tbsp fresh lemon juice
- 2 fat garlic cloves, smashed
- 1 tsp dried oregano
- Coarse sea salt and ground black pepper, to taste

1. Toss the squid with the remaining ingredients in a glass or ceramic bowl; cover and let it marinate for about 1 hour.
2. Add the squid rings to both drawers.
3. Select zone 1 and pair it with "ROAST" at 200°C for 10 minutes. Select "MATCH" followed by the "START / STOP" button.
4. When zone 1 time reaches 5 minutes, turn the squid rings over, baste them with the reserved marinade and continue to cook for 5 minutes more.
5. Serve with your favourite Mediterranean salad, if desired. Bon appétit!

ROAST FISH WITH SALSA ROMESCO

Serves 4
Prep time: 10 minutes
Cook time: 16 minutes

Per Serving:
Calories: 334
Fat: 15.4g
Carbs: 28.4g
Fiber: 3.9g
Protein: 22.1g

- 400g cod fillet
- 2 fat garlic cloves, smashed
- Coarse sea salt and ground black pepper, to taste
- 1 tsp olive oil
- 2 tsp fresh lemon juice
- 100g plain flour

Salsa Romesco:
- 2 red peppers, whole
- 1 garlic clove, crushed
- 1 red chilli, deseeded and finely chopped
- 50g blanched almonds, roughly crushed
- 1 tbsp paprika
- 200g passata (tomato paste)
- 2 tbsp extra-virgin olive oil

1. Pat the fish dry with tea towels. Then, toss the fish fillets with lemon juice, garlic, plain flour, salt, black pepper, and 1 teaspoon of olive oil. Place the fish in the zone 1 drawer.
2. Brush the peppers with cooking oil. Place the peppers in the zone 2 drawer.
3. Select zone 1 and pair it with "AIR FRY" at 200°C for 8 minutes. Select zone 2 and pair it with "ROAST" at 200°C for 16 minutes. Select "SYNC" followed by the "START / STOP" button.
4. In a blender, place the peppers along with the other salsa ingredients. Blend until creamy, uniform, and smooth.
5. Serve roast fish with a fresh Salsa Romesco on the side and enjoy!

GREEK FISH TRAYBAKE

Serves 4
Prep time: 10 minutes
Cook time: 20 minutes

Per Serving:
Calories: 234
Fat: 4.4g
Carbs: 17.9g
Fiber: 2g
Protein: 29g

- 500g salmon fillets
- 200g carrots, cleaned and quartered
- 200g potatoes, peeled and cut into bite-sized pieces
- 1 large leek, quartered
- 1 tsp Italian spice mix
- 1 tbsp olive oil
- Sea salt and ground black pepper, to taste
- 100ml fish broth

1. Toss the fish and vegetables with the spices and olive oil. Place the fish in the zone 1 drawer (with a crisper plate).
2. Then, place the vegetables and fish broth in a lightly oiled baking tray. Add the baking tray to the zone 2 drawer.
3. Select zone 1 and pair it with "AIR FRY" at 200°C for 8 minutes. Select zone 2 and pair it with "AIR FRY" at 200°C for 20 minutes. Select "SYNC" followed by the "START / STOP" button.
4. Serve the fish and vegetables in the tray and enjoy!

CRAB AND POTATO CROQUETTES

Serves 8
Prep time: 10 minutes
Cook time: 33 minutes

Per Serving:
Calories: 365
Fat: 6g
Carbs: 53.3g
Fiber: 3.3g
Protein: 21.2g

- 800g white potatoes, peeled and diced
- 2 tbsp olive oil
- Sea salt and ground black pepper, to your liking
- 2 spring onions, finely chopped
- 600g crabmeat
- 1 tsp dried dill
- 1 tsp lemon zest
- 2 medium egg, beaten
- 1 tsp red pepper flakes
- 1 tsp dried parsley flakes
- 200g plain flour
- 200g breadcrumbs

1. Toss the potatoes with 1 teaspoon of olive oil, salt, and pepper.
2. Place the potatoes in both drawers and cook them at 190 degrees C for about 10 minutes; shake the basket and continue cooking for a further 10 minutes, until they are just tender.
3. Push the potatoes through a ricer. Stir in the crabmeat, along with the other ingredients.
4. Shape the mixture into balls and flatten them slightly with a fork. Place the croquettes in both drawers.
5. Select zone 1 and pair it with "AIR FRY" at 180°C for 13 minutes. Select "MATCH" followed by the "START / STOP" button.
6. When zone 1 time reaches 7 minutes, turn them over to promote even cooking.

Bon appétit!

FISH EN PAPILLOTE

Serves 4
Prep time: 10 minutes
Cook time: 14 minutes

Per Serving:
Calories: 443
Fat: 10.1g
Carbs: 2.3g
Fiber: 3g
Protein: 80g

- 4 (180g) mackerel fillets, skin-on
- 2 shallots, peeled and cut into wedges
- 2 large carrots, trimmed and sliced
- 2 medium celeriac roots, trimmed, peeled, and sliced
- 2 medium bell peppers, seeded and sliced
- 2 tsp olive oil
- Sea salt and freshly ground black pepper, to taste
- 4 fat garlic cloves, sliced
- 1 tsp paprika

1. Pat the fish dry using paper towels. Tear off 4 squares of parchment.
2. Assemble the packets: Place the fish fillet in the centre of one side of the parchment paper. Top the fish with the other ingredients.
3. Now, create a half-moon shape with the parchment paper, folding as you go and sealing the food inside. Place the pockets in both drawers.
4. Select zone 1 and pair it with "AIR FRY" at 190°C for 14 minutes. Select "MATCH" followed by the "START / STOP" button.
5. When zone 1 time reaches 7 minutes, open the pockets and continue to cook for a further 7 minutes.

Bon appétit!

AROMATIC GARLIC COD

Serves 8
Prep time: 10 minutes
Cook time: 11 minutes

Per Serving:
Calories: 154
Fat: 4g
Carbs: 3.3g
Fiber: 0.9g
Protein: 26g

- 4 fat garlic cloves, smashed
- 1 tsp dried rosemary
- 1 tsp dried thyme
- 1 tsp dried sage
- 1 tbsp paprika
- 1200g cod fillets
- Coarse sea salt and ground black pepper, to taste
- 2 tbsp olive oil

1. Crush the garlic, herbs, and spices using a mortar and pestle; add olive oil and stir to combine.
2. Rub the fish with the freshly prepared garlic herb mixture.
3. Select zone 1 and pair it with "AIR FRY" at 200°C for 11 minutes. Select "MATCH" followed by the "START / STOP" button.
4. Serve immediately and enjoy!

SALMON STEAKS WITH HORSERADISH SAUCE

Serves 8
Prep time: 10 minutes
Cook time: 14 minutes

Per Serving:
Calories: 214
Fat: 12.4g
Carbs: 1.9g
Fiber: 0.5g
Protein: 21.6g

- 800g salmon steaks, 2 cm thick
- Sea salt and ground black pepper, to taste
- 1 tbsp olive oil
- 100ml plain yoghurt
- 80g aioli
- 2 tsp horseradish

1. Pat the salmon steaks dry with tea (kitchen) towels and rub them with salt, pepper, and olive oil. Transfer the salmon steaks to both drawers.
2. Select zone 1 and pair it with "ROAST" at 200°C for 14 minutes. Select "MATCH" followed by the "START / STOP" button.
3. In the meantime, whisk the remaining ingredients to make the horseradish sauce. Serve warm salmon steaks with horseradish sauce.

Bon appétit!

FISH FINGERS

Serves 4
Prep time: 10 minutes
Cook time: 12 minutes

Per Serving:
Calories: 311
Fat: 10.2g
Carbs: 25.6g
Fiber: 1.5g
Protein: 27.6g

- 1kgg cod fillets
- 10g plain flour
- 100g parmesan cheese, grated
- 1 tsp dried oregano
- 1 tsp dried basil
- 1 tsp cayenne pepper
- Sea salt and ground black pepper, to taste
- 2 tbsp olive oil
- 1 large egg, whisked
- 180g tortilla chips, crushed
- 1 tbsp dried parsley flakes

1. Rinse the fish and pat it dry using tea towels. Then, cut the fish into strips.
2. Then, whisk the egg and flour in a shallow bowl. Now, combine the tortilla chips, cheese, and spices in another shallow bowl.
3. Dip the fish strips in the egg / flour mixture, then, roll them over the chip / parmesan mixture.
4. Transfer fish fingers to both drawers. Brush fish fingers with olive oil.
5. Select zone 1 and pair it with "ROAST" at 200°C for 12 minutes. Select "MATCH" followed by the "START / STOP" button.
6. Make sure to flip them over halfway through to ensure even browning.
7. Serve immediately and enjoy!

OLD BAY SCALLOPS

Serves 6
Prep time: 10 minutes
Cook time: 8 minutes

Per Serving:
Calories: 190
Fat: 5.5g
Carbs: 8.2g
Fiber: 0.5g
Protein: 24.2g

- 1200g sea scallops
- 2 tbsp fresh lemon juice
- 2 tbsp white cooking wine
- 2 tsp olive oil
- 1 tbsp Old Bay spice mix
- Coarse sea salt, to taste

1. Rub the scallops with the other ingredients; arrange them in both drawers.
2. Select zone 1 and pair it with "AIR FRY" at 200°C for 8 minutes. Select "MATCH" followed by the "START / STOP" button.
3. Make sure to flip them over halfway through to ensure even browning.
4. Serve your scallops with a fresh Mediterranean salad of choice.
Bon appétit!

FISHERMAN'S TIGER PRAWNS

Serves 4
Prep time: 10 minutes
Cook time: 12 minutes

Per Serving:
Calories: 185
Fat: 5.4g
Carbs: 5.1g
Fiber: 0.2g
Protein: 26.2g

- 600g tiger prawns, peeled and deveined
- 1 tbsp Cajun spice mix
- 50g polenta
- 1 garlic clove, crushed
- 1 tbsp lemon juice
- 1 tbsp dried basil
- 1 tbsp dried rosemary
- 1 tbsp olive oil

1. Toss your prawns with spices, polenta, garlic, lemon juice, and herbs.
2. Brush your prawns with olive oil and lower them into both drawers.
3. Select zone 1 and pair it with "AIR FRY" at 200°C for 12 minutes. Select "MATCH" followed by the "START / STOP" button.
4. Make sure to shake the basket halfway through the cooking time to ensure even browning.
5. Serve warm and enjoy!

PARMESAN CRUSTED FISH

Serves 6
Prep time: 10 minutes
Cook time: 12 minutes

Per Serving:
Calories: 414
Fat: 18.2g
Carbs: 20.4g
Fiber: 0.9g
Protein: 40.2g

- 1kg cod fillet, skinless (or any type of firm white fish)
- 160g breadcrumbs
- 2 tsp fresh lemon juice
- 100g grated parmesan
- 2 tbsp parsley, chopped
- Sea salt and ground black pepper, to taste
- 1 tsp olive oil

1. Pat the fish dry with tea towels.
2. Mix the breadcrumbs with the lemon juice, parmesan, chopped parsley, salt, and back pepper.
3. Cover the fish with the breadcrumb / parmesan mixture.
4. Select zone 1 and pair it with "AIR FRY" at 200°C for 12 minutes. Select "MATCH" followed by the "START / STOP" button.
5. Make sure to turn the fish fillets over halfway through the cooking time to ensure even browning.
6. Serve with your favourite side dish and enjoy!

MEDITERRANEAN FISH GRATIN

Serves 8
Prep time: 10 minutes
Cook time: 23 minutes

Per Serving:
Calories: 346
Fat: 12.4g
Carbs: 27.5g
Fiber: 4.4g
Protein: 32.3g

- 1kg skinless cod fillets, sliced into strips
- 250g fennel bulb, trimmed and thinly sliced
- 24 fat garlic cloves, finely sliced
- 1 large red onion, thinly sliced
- 2 (400g) cans Mediterranean tomatoes with herbs, chopped
- A large bunch of flat-leaf or Italian parsley, roughly chopped
- 2 tbsp olive oil
- 160g finely grated parmesan
- 100g coarse dried breadcrumbs

1. Stir the fish, fennel, garlic, red onion, tomatoes, parsley, and olive oil into two lightly oiled casserole dishes.
2. Select zone 1 and pair it with "BAKE" at 190°C for 23 minutes. Select "MATCH" followed by the "START / STOP" button.
3. When zone 1 time reaches 15 minutes, remove the casserole dishes from the cooking basket and add the cheese and breadcrumbs.
4. Now, continue to bake for a further 8 minutes, until the gratins are golden brown and bubbling on the top.

Bon appétit!

EASY FRIED SCAMPI WITH PARSNIPS

Serves 4
Prep time: 10 minutes
Cook time: 14 minutes

Per Serving:
Calories: 249
Fat: 3.5g
Carbs: 23.6g
Fiber: 0.6g
Protein: 5.5g

- 10 langoustines (or Dublin Bay prawn tails)
- 90g polenta
- Sea salt and ground black pepper, to taste
- 1 tbsp Italian spice mix
- 2 tsp olive oil
- 400g parsnips, peel and cut into 1.5cm lengths

1. Mix polenta with spices in a shallow dish.
2. Pat the scampi dry with tea towels; toss them in the polenta mixture.
3. Place your scampi in the zone 1 drawer. Spray langoustine with 1 teaspoon of olive oil.
4. Toss the parsnip with the remaining 1 teaspoon of olive oil. Place them in the zone 2 drawer.
5. Select zone 1 and pair it with "AIR FRY" at 180°C for 12 minutes. Select zone 2 and pair it with "ROAST" at 200°C for 14 minutes. Select "SYNC" followed by the "START / STOP" button.
6. Serve with hot gnocchi, if desired. Bon appétit!

CRAB AND CAULIFLOWER PATTIES

Serves 8
Prep time: 10 minutes
Cook time: 14 minutes

Per Serving:
Calories: 293
Fat: 6.5g
Carbs: 38.1g
Fiber: 3.3g
Protein: 19.7g

- 800g cauliflower, grated
- 520g crabmeat
- 2 tbsp olive oil
- 2 spring onions, finely chopped
- 1 tsp red pepper flakes
- 180g plain flour
- 2 medium eggs, beaten
- 200g breadcrumbs
- Coarse sea salt and ground black pepper, to taste

1. Add a crisper plate to the cooking basket.
2. Mix all the ingredients in a bowl. Shape the mixture into small balls.
3. Lower the balls onto lightly oiled crisper plates and flatten them with a fork; brush the patties with cooking oil.
4. Select zone 1 and pair it with "AIR FRY" at 180°C for 14 minutes. Select "MATCH" followed by the "START / STOP" button.
5. When zone 1 time reaches 7 minutes, turn the patties over and reinsert the drawers to resume cooking.

Bon appétit!

EASY SCALLOPS WITH ROAST PEPPER SALAD

Serves 6
Prep time: 10 minutes
Cook time: 15 minutes

Per Serving:
Calories: 218
Fat: 8.5g
Carbs: 14.9g
Fiber: 1.3g
Protein: 22g

- 1kg sea scallops
- 1 fat garlic clove, peeled
- 1 tbsp olive oil
- 1 sprig thyme

- 1 tbsp whole peppercorns
- 1 small lemon, freshly squeezed
- 1 tsp mustard seeds
- Coarse sea salt, to taste

Roast Pepper Salad:
- 4 bell peppers, whole
- 1 fat garlic clove, peeled
- Sea salt and ground black pepper, to taste
- 2 tbsp extra-virgin olive oil
- 2 tbsp Mediterranean red wine vinegar

1. Add a crisper plate to the cooking basket.
2. Crush the garlic, herbs, and spices using a mortar and pestle; add olive oil and lemon juice; stir to combine.
3. Rub the scallops with the freshly prepared herb mixture. Now, add the scallops to the zone 1 drawer and peppers to the zone 2 drawer.
4. Select zone 1 and pair it with "AIR FRY" at 200°C for 8 minutes. Select zone 2 and pair it with "ROAST" at 200°C for 15 minutes. Select "SYNC" followed by the "START / STOP" button.
5. Cut the peppers into halves and toss them with the other salad ingredients.
6. Serve your scallops with roast pepper salad on the side. Enjoy!

SUNDAY FISH CASSEROLE

Serves 7
Prep time: 10 minutes
Cook time: 20 minutes

Per Serving:
Calories: 282
Fat: 13.3g
Carbs: 8.9g
Fiber: 2g
Protein: 30.3g

- 1kg sole fillets (or any white fish), sliced
- 1 large leek, sliced
- 400g medium cremini mushrooms, quarter
- 5 medium ripe tomatoes, deseeded, skin removed, and roughly chopped
- 2 tbsp olive oil
- Sea salt and ground black pepper, to taste
- 1 tbsp Italian spice mix
- 200g creamy feta cheese

1. Simply toss the fish, leeks, mushrooms, tomatoes, olive oil, and spices into two lightly oiled casserole dishes.
2. Select zone 1 and pair it with "BAKE" at 190°C for 20 minutes. Select "MATCH" followed by the "START / STOP" button.
3. When zone 1 time reaches 10 minutes, remove the casserole dishes from the cooking basket and add the cheese.
4. Now, continue to bake for a further 10 minutes, until the tops are golden brown and bubbling.

Bon appétit!

FISH AND SWEETCORN CAKES

Serves 6
Prep time: 10 minutes
Cook time: 34 minutes

Per Serving:
Calories: 426
Fat: 13.6g
Carbs: 47g
Fiber: 4.9g
Protein: 28.2g

- 800g white potatoes, peeled and diced
- 1 tbsp olive oil
- Sea salt and ground black pepper, to taste
- 3 (185g) cans of tuna in water, drained
- 300g canned sweetcorn, cream-style, drained
- A small bunch of chives, snipped
- A small bunch of parsley, roughly chopped
- 1 large egg, beaten
- 160g dried breadcrumb
- 4 tbsp mayonnaise

1. Toss the potatoes with 1 teaspoon of olive oil, salt, and pepper.
2. Place the potatoes in both drawers and cook them at 190 degrees C for about 10 minutes; shake the basket and continue cooking for a further 10 minutes, until they are just tender.
3. Push the potatoes through a ricer. Stir in the other ingredients and shape the mixture into small patties.
4. Arrange the patties on crisper plates in the zone 1 and 2 drawers.
5. Select zone 1 and pair it with "AIR FRY" at 180°C for 14 minutes. Select "MATCH" followed by the "START / STOP" button.

Bon appétit!

PESTO AND OLIVE CRUSTED HADDOCK

Serves 8
Prep time: 10 minutes
Cook time: 12 minutes

Per Serving:
Calories: 249
Fat: 8.5g
Carbs: 14.8g
Fiber: 1.2g
Protein: 28.2g

- 1200g haddock fillets, skinless (or any type of firm white fish)
- 200g breadcrumbs
- 4 tbsp green pesto
- 20 green olives, stoned and roughly chopped
- Finely grated zest of 1 large lemon
- Sea salt and ground black pepper, to taste
- 2 tsp olive oil

1. Pat the fish dry with tea towels.
2. Mix the other ingredients until everything is well combined. Cover the fish with the pesto
olive mixture.
3. Lower the fish onto lightly oiled crisper plates in the zone 1 and 2 drawers.
4. Select zone 1 and pair it with "AIR FRY" at 200°C for 12 minutes. Select "MATCH" followed by the "START / STOP" button.
5. Make sure to turn the fish fillets over halfway through the cooking time to ensure even cooking.

Bon appétit!

PAPRIKA SALMON WITH PORTOBELLO MUSHROOMS

Serves 6
Prep time: 10 minutes
Cook time: 16 minutes

Per Serving:
Calories: 328
Fat: 13.9g
Carbs: 6.5g
Fiber: 2.4g
Protein: 42.3g

- 1.2kg salmon steaks
- 600g Portobello mushrooms, whole
- 2 tsp fresh lemon juice
- 2 fat garlic cloves, smashed
- 1 tbsp Spanish paprika
- 1 tsp dried rosemary
- 1 tsp dried oregano
- 1 tsp dried basil
- 1 tbsp paprika
- Coarse sea salt and ground black pepper, to taste
- 2 tbsp olive oil

1. Toss the salmon steaks and Portobello mushrooms with lemon juice, garlic, spices and olive oil.
2. Add crisper plates to both drawers; brush the crisper plates with the cooking oil of your choice.
3. Add the salmon steaks to the zone 1 drawer and Portobello mushrooms to the zone 2 drawer.
4. Select zone 1 and pair it with "ROAST" at 200°C for 16 minutes. Select zone 2 and pair it with "ROAST" at 180°C for 12 minutes. Select "SYNC" followed by the "START / STOP" button.
5. Eat warm and enjoy!

STUFFED TOMATOES WITH TUNA

Serves 4
Prep time: 10 minutes
Cook time: 12 minutes

Per Serving:
Calories: 484
Fat: 26g
Carbs: 20.8g
Fiber: 4g
Protein: 43.4g

- 4 large tomatoes (beefsteak or heirloom)
- 400g canned tuna in oil, drained and roughly flaked
- 100g green olives, stoned and chopped
- 1 large red onion, chopped
- Cracked black pepper, to taste
- 1 tsp garlic granules
- 200g parmesan cheese, preferably freshly grated

1. Slice the tops off the tomatoes. Then, scoop out the seeds and pulp from them, discarding the central cores.
2. In a bowl, mix the canned tuna, olives, onion, black pepper, and garlic granules. Divide the tuna mixture between the prepared tomatoes.
3. Lower the tomatoes into both drawers.
4. Select zone 1 and pair it with "AIR FRY" at 190°C for 12 minutes. Select "MATCH" followed by the "START / STOP" button.
5. When zone 1 time reaches 6 minutes, top them with cheese and continue to cook for a further 6 minutes, until cooked through.

CHAPTER 4
POULTRY

CHICKEN THIGHS AND BRUSSELS SPROUT TRAYBAKE

Serves 6
Prep time: 10 minutes
Cook time: 16 minutes

Per Serving:
Calories: 440
Fat: 29.9g
Carbs: 12.7g
Fiber: 5.3g
Protein: 31.3g

- 1kg chicken thighs, boneless and skinless
- 2 cloves garlic, smashed
- 400ml tomato purée
- 1 tbsp red wine vinegar
- Sea salt and ground black pepper, to taste
- 2 thyme sprigs
- 1 rosemary sprig
- 2 tsp olive oil
- 600g Brussels sprouts, trimmed and quartered

1. Toss the chicken thighs, garlic, tomato purée, vinegar, spices, and 1 teaspoon of olive oil in a lightly-greased roasting tin. Lower the roasting tin into the zone 1 drawer.
2. Add the Brussels sprouts to the zone 2 drawer (with a crisper plate). Brush the Brussels sprouts with the remaining 1 teaspoon of olive oil.
3. Select zone 1 and pair it with "ROAST" at 200°C for 16 minutes. Select zone 2 and pair it with "ROAST" at 200°C for 13 minutes. Select "SYNC" followed by the "START / STOP" button.
4. Place the Brussels sprouts in the tin and serve. Bon appétit!

CLASSIC TURKEY SALAD

Serves 8
Prep time: 10 minutes
Cook time: 55 minutes

Per Serving:
Calories: 310
Fat: 14g
Carbs: 4.6g
Fiber: 1.1g
Protein: 28.3g

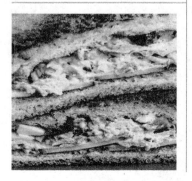

- 1kg turkey breast, boneless and skinless
- 2 large bell peppers, deseeded and sliced
- 2 tbsp olive oil
- 1 tsp garlic granules
- Sea salt and ground black pepper, to taste
- 4 tbsp extra-virgin olive oil
- 1 large cucumber, sliced
- 1 large tomato, diced
- A small handful of fresh basil leaves, roughly chopped

1. Toss the turkey breast and bell peppers with olive oil and spices. Place the turkey breast in the zone 1 drawer and the peppers in the zone 2 drawer.
2. Select zone 1 and pair it with "ROAST" at 180°C for 55 minutes. Select zone 2 and pair it with "ROAST" at 200°C for 13 minutes. Select "SYNC" followed by the "START / STOP" button.
3. Now, cut the turkey and peppers into strips; toss them with the other ingredients in a nice salad bowl.
Bon appétit!

OLD-FASHIONED ITALIAN CASSEROLE

Serves 8
Prep time: 10 minutes
Cook time: 30 minutes

Per Serving:
Calories: 424
Fat: 26.5g
Carbs: 8.1g
Fiber: 1.7g
Protein: 37.3g

- 200ml tomato passata
- 10.2g chicken drumsticks, skinless, boneless, and sliced into strips
- 2 tbsp olive oil
- 1 tbsp Italian herb mix
- 1 large red onion, thinly sliced
- 2 fat garlic cloves, minced
- 4 bell peppers, thinly sliced
- 400g Cremini mushrooms, sliced
- 200ml chicken stock
- 200g goat cheese, crumbled

1. Remove a crisper plate from your Ninja Dual Zone Air Fryer.
2. Spoon the passata into the bottom of two lightly greased baking trays.
3. Add the other ingredients, except the cheese, to the baking trays; gently stir to combine.
4. Select zone 1 and pair it with "BAKE" at 180°C for 30 minutes. Select "MATCH" followed by the "START / STOP" button.
5. When zone 1 time reaches 20 minutes, top your casserole with cheese and continue to cook for a further 10 minutes, until cooked through.

Bon appétit!

ROTISSERIE-STYLE ROAST CHICKEN

Serves 6
Prep time: 10 minutes
Cook time: 16 minutes

Per Serving:
Calories: 394
Fat: 19.5g
Carbs: 1.3g
Fiber: 0.3g
Protein: 53g

- 1.2kg chicken breasts, skinless and boneless
- 1 tsp Italian spice mix
- 2 fat garlic cloves, smashed
- Sea salt and ground black pepper, to taste
- 2 tbsp olive oil

1. Rub the chicken with the other ingredients until it is well-coated on all sides.
2. Lower the chicken breast into both drawers.
3. Select zone 1 and pair it with "BAKE" at 200°C for 16 minutes. Select "MATCH" followed by the "START / STOP" button.
4. Transfer the chicken to a cutting board and leave it to rest for about 10 minutes before carving and serving.

Enjoy!

CLASSIC CHICKEN SANDWICH

Serves 6
Prep time: 10 minutes
Cook time: 15 minutes

Per Serving:
Calories: 543
Fat: 24.5g
Carbs: 28.4g
Fiber: 3g
Protein: 54.1g

- 1kg chicken breasts, skinless
- 1 tsp hot paprika
- Sea salt and ground black pepper, to taste
- 1 tbsp olive oil
- 6 sandwich rolls
- 1 large head of lettuce
- 1 large tomato, diced
- 200g feta cheese, crumbled

1. Toss the chicken with the spices and olive oil in a resalable bag; toss until the chicken is well coated on all sides.
2. Lower the chicken (breast side down) into the lightly oiled drawers.
3. Select zone 1 and pair it with "AIR FRY" at 190°C for 15 minutes. Select "MATCH" followed by the "START / STOP" button.
4. Allow the chicken to rest for about 10 minutes on a cutting board.
5. Cut the chicken into bite-sized slices and discard the bones. Assemble your sandwiches with sandwich rolls, chicken, lettuce, tomato, and feta.

Bon appétit!

ROAST TURKEY WITH POTATOES

Serves 8
Prep time: 10 minutes
Cook time: 55 minutes

Per Serving:
Calories: 349
Fat: 12.5g
Carbs: 27.5g
Fiber: 2.8g
Protein: 30.3g

- 1kg turkey breasts, boneless and skinless
- 2 tbsp olive oil
- 1kg white potatoes, peeled and diced
- 1 tsp Aleppo pepper
- 1 tsp garlic granules
- Sea salt and ground black pepper, to taste
- 1 rosemary sprig
- 1 tbsp basil leaves, roughly chopped

1. Toss turkey and potatoes with the other ingredients. Add the turkey to a lightly greased roasting tin. Add the potatoes to another roasting tin.
2. Lower the roasting tins into both drawers.
3. Select zone 1 and pair it with "ROAST" at 180°C for 55 minutes. Select zone 2 and pair it with "ROAST" at 190°C for 20 minutes. Select "SYNC" followed by the "START / STOP" button.

Bon appétit!

SPICED CHICKEN SALAD

Serves 8
Prep time: 10 minutes
Cook time: 18 minutes

Per Serving:
Calories: 315
Fat: 17.3g
Carbs: 11.1g
Fiber: 2.2g
Protein: 29.2g

- 1kg chicken breasts
- 600g courgette, sliced
- 3 tbsp extra-virgin olive oil
- Sea salt and ground black pepper, to taste
- 1 large red onion, sliced
- 1 large Greek cucumber, sliced
- 4 bell peppers, deseeded and sliced
- 1 Aleppo pepper, deseeded and sliced

1. Toss the chicken with 1 teaspoon of olive oil, salt, and black pepper to taste. Lower the chicken into the zone 1 drawer.
2. Toss courgette with 1 teaspoon of olive oil, salt, and black pepper. Add courgette slices to the zone 2 drawer.
3. Select zone 1 and pair it with "ROAST" at 190°C for 18 minutes. Select zone 2 and pair it with "ROAST" at 200°C for 9 minutes. Select "SYNC" followed by the "START / STOP" button.
4. In a salad bowl, gently stir the chicken and courgette slices with the other ingredients. Enjoy!

CHICKEN AND ONION TRAYBAKE

Serves 6
Prep time: 10 minutes
Cook time: 16 minutes

Per Serving:
Calories: 457
Fat: 32.3g
Carbs: 11.6g
Fiber: 2.5g
Protein: 29.3g

- 1kg chicken thighs, boneless and skinless
- 2 cloves garlic, smashed
- Sea salt and ground black pepper, to taste
- 1 rosemary sprig
- 2 tbsp olive oil
- 4 medium onions, halved
- 4 medium ripe tomatoes

1. Toss the chicken thighs with 1 tablespoon of olive oil, garlic, and spices in a lightly greased roasting tin. Lower the roasting tin into the zone 1 drawer.
2. Toss the onions and tomatoes with 1 tablespoon of olive oil and spices in a lightly greased roasting tin. Lower the roasting tin into the zone 2 drawer.
3. Select zone 1 and pair it with "ROAST" at 200°C for 16 minutes. Select zone 2 and pair it with "ROAST" at 190°C for 10 minutes. Select "SYNC" followed by the "START / STOP" button.
4. Serve the chicken and vegetables in the tin.
Bon appétit!

CHICKEN WITH GNOCCHI

Serves 8
Prep time: 10 minutes
Cook time: 20 minutes

Per Serving:
Calories: 489
Fat: 32.6g
Carbs: 16.2g
Fiber: 1.9g
Protein: 30g

- 1kg chicken thighs, skinless and boneless
- 2 tsp olive oil
- 1 tbsp paprika
- Sea salt and ground black pepper, to taste
- 400g dry potato gnocchi
- 1 large red onion, sliced
- 4 tbsp Kalamata olives, stoned and sliced
- 1 tbsp garlic, minced
- 200ml vegetable broth
- 2 large tomatoes, chopped
- 200g parmesan cheese, grated

1. Cut the chicken thighs into bite-sized pieces and place them in two lightly greased roasting tins. Add the other ingredients, except the parmesan cheese, and gently stir to combine.
2. Lower the roasting tins into both drawers.
3. Select zone 1 and pair it with "BAKE" at 195°C for 20 minutes. Select "MATCH" followed by the "START / STOP" button.
4. When zone 1 time reaches 10 minutes, top your casseroles with cheese and continue to cook for a further 10 minutes, until cooked through.

Bon appétit!

TURKEY AND VEGETABLE TRAYBAKE

Serves 8
Prep time: 10 minutes
Cook time: 55 minutes

Per Serving:
Calories: 301
Fat: 14.5g
Carbs: 6.4g
Fiber: 1.5g
Protein: 34.3g

- 1.2kg turkey breast, boneless and skinless
- 2 tbsp olive oil
- 1 large red onion, halved
- 2 large carrots, quartered
- 400g ripe tomatoes, quartered
- Sea salt and ground black pepper, to taste
- 1 rosemary sprig
- 1 tbsp basil leaves, roughly chopped
- 4 cloves garlic, sliced

1. Toss turkey breasts and vegetables with spices, garlic, and olive oil in a lightly greased roasting tin.
2. Add turkey breasts to a lightly oiled roasting tin. Add the vegetables to another roasting tin.
3. Lower the roasting tins into both drawers.
4. Select zone 1 and pair it with "ROAST" at 180°C for 55 minutes. Select zone 2 and pair it with "ROAST" at 200°C for 16 minutes. Select "SYNC" followed by the "START / STOP" button.
5. Serve straight from the tin and eat with your favourite Mediterranean salad. Bon appétit!

LAYERED CHICKEN BAKE

Serves 8
Prep time: 10 minutes
Cook time: 35 minutes

Per Serving:
Calories: 366
Fat: 14.3g
Carbs: 21.4g
Fiber: 1.5g
Protein: 36.3g

- 1kg chicken, skinless and boneless, cut into bite-sized pieces
- Sea salt and ground black pepper, to taste   • 1 tbsp olive oil
- 6 medium pita breads   • 200g parmesan cheese, grated
Sauce:
- 1 tbsp olive oil   • 1 tsp Italian spice mix
- 200ml marinara   • 200ml vegetable broth
- 1 tsp Aleppo pepper, deveined and minced

1. Insert crisper plates in zone 1 and 2 drawers. Spray the crisper plates with nonstick cooking oil.
2. Toss the chicken with salt, black pepper, and olive oil. Divide the chicken pieces between both drawers.
3. Select zone 1 and pair it with "ROAST" at 200°C for 20 minutes. Select "MATCH" to duplicate settings across both zones. Press the "START / STOP" button.
4. At the halfway point, gently flip the meat and reinsert the drawers to resume cooking.
5. Meanwhile, mix all the sauce ingredients until well combined. Divide the chicken between tortillas; top with 100 grams of cheese and roll them tightly.
6. Divide these rolls between two lightly greased baking tins; spoon the sauce over them and sprinkle over the remaining 100 grams of grated cheese; add them to both drawers (without crisper plates).
7. Select zone 1 and pair it with "BAKE" at 190°C for 15 minutes, until golden brown on the top. Select "MATCH" to duplicate settings across both zones. Press the "START / STOP" button. Bon appétit!

HARISSA DUCK BREASTS

Serves 6
Prep time: 10 minutes
Cook time: 22 minutes

Per Serving:
Calories: 306
Fat: 14.3g
Carbs: 6.4g
Fiber: 0.5g
Protein: 36.3g

- 1.2 kg duck breasts, boneless   • 100ml Harissa sauce
- 1 tbsp sesame oil   • 1 tbsp clear Mediterrane honey
- 10g ginger, peeled and finely grated
- Sea salt, to taste

1. In a mixing bowl, toss the duck breasts with the other ingredients. Add the breasts to the cooking basket.
2. Select zone 1 and pair it with "AIR FRY" at 200°C for 22 minutes. Select "MATCH" to duplicate settings across both zones. Press the "START / STOP" button.
3. When zone 1 time reaches 11 minutes, turn the duck breasts over and baste with the remaining sauce. Reinsert the drawers to resume cooking.
4. Serve warm duck breasts with a fresh Mediterranean salad of your choice. Bon appétit!

ONE-PAN CHICKEN RISOTTO

Serves 6
Prep time: 10 minutes
Cook time: 30 minutes

Per Serving:
Calories: 346
Fat: 10.3g
Carbs: 23.4g
Fiber: 4.3g
Protein: 36.3g

- 1000g chicken, boneless and skinless, chopped
- 1 onion, chopped   • 300ml vegetable broth
- 1 (400g) can tomatoes, chopped
- 2 garlic cloves, crushed or finely chopped
- 2 tbsp olive oil   • 350g cooked rice
- 200g frozen green peas, thawed   • 1 heaped tsp Aleppo pepper
- 1 thyme sprig, leaves finely chopped
- 1 rosemary sprig, leaves finely chopped

1. In a mixing bowl, thoroughly combine the chicken, onion, and vegetable broth. Divide the mixture between two baking tins. Add baking tins to the drawers (without crisper plates).
2. Select zone 1 and pair it with "AIR FRY" at 190°C for 15 minutes. Select "MATCH" to duplicate settings across both zones. Press the "START / STOP" button. At the halfway point, stir the mixture with a wooden spoon and reinsert the drawers to resume cooking.
3. Once cooked, add the other ingredients to the baking tins. Gently stir to combine.
4. Select zone 1 and pair it with "ROAST" at 190°C for 15 minutes. Select "MATCH" to duplicate settings across both zones. Press the "START / STOP" button.
5. Serve warm and enjoy!

MEDITERRANEAN HERB CHICKEN PASTA BAKE

Serves 6
Prep time: 10 minutes
Cook time: 24 minutes

Per Serving:
Calories: 566
Fat: 24.6g
Carbs: 40.4g
Fiber: 6.5g
Protein: 47.6g

- 250g dry whole-wheat pasta of choice
- 800g chicken breasts, skinless, sliced into strips
- 2 tbsp olive oil   • 1 large onion, finely chopped
- 2 fat garlic cloves, crushed • 2 (400g) cans tomatoes, chopped
- 1 tsp Aleppo pepper   • Sea salt and ground black pepper, to taste
- 1 tbsp fresh parsley, chopped • 1 tbsp fresh coriander, chopped
- 200g Provolone cheese, grated

1. Remove a crisper plate from your Ninja Dual Zone Air Fryer. Brush two baking tins with nonstick oil.
2. Cook your pasta according to the package instructions.
3. In the meantime, heat olive oil in a nonstick frying pan over a medium-high flame. Cook the chicken for about 4 minutes, until they are no longer pink.
4. Add the chicken to the pasta; stir through the onion, garlic, tomatoes, spices, and 100 grams of cheese. Spoon the mixture into the prepared baking tins; now, add the tins to your Ninja Dual Zone Air Fryer.
5. Select zone 1 and pair it with "BAKE" at 180°C for 20 minutes. Select "MATCH" followed by the "START / STOP" button.
6. When zone 1 time reaches 10 minutes, top with the remaining 100 grams of Provolone cheese; reinsert the drawers to continue cooking.

Bon appétit!

PARMESAN MEATLOAF CUPS WITH OLIVES

Serves 9
Prep time: 10 minutes
Cook time: 20 minutes

Per Serving:
Calories: 286
Fat: 13.1g
Carbs: 17.4g
Fiber: 2.2g
Protein: 25.6g

- 1kg turkey mince
- 1 large egg, beaten
- 1 medium onion, chopped
- 2 garlic cloves, minced
- 1 large bell pepper, seeded and chopped
- 160g fresh breadcrumbs
- 100g green olives, stoned and chopped
- 1 tbsp Mediterranean herb mix
- 1 tbsp olive oil
- 200ml marinara
- 1 tbsp dried mustard
- 1 tbsp clear Mediterranean honey

1. Brush 9 muffin cases with nonstick cooking oil.
2. Mix the turkey mince, egg, onion, garlic, bell pepper, breadcrumbs, olives, Mediterranean herbs, and olive oil until everything is well incorporated.
3. Mix the marinara with mustard and honey.
4. Press the turkey mince mixture into the prepared muffin cases. Place them in both drawers.
5. Select zone 1 and pair it with "AIR FRY" at 180°C for 20 minutes. Select "MATCH" to duplicate settings across both zones. Press the "START / STOP" button.
6. When zone 1 time reaches 10 minutes, spread the tomato mixture over the meatloaf cups and bake for a further 10 minutes, until the centre of your meatloaf reaches 74°C.
7. Reinsert the drawers to continue cooking. Bon appétit!

CHAPTER 5
GRAINS & LEGUMES

MEDITERRANEAN MILLET AND BEAN CAKES

Serves 7
Prep time: 10 minutes
Cook time: 20 minutes

Per Serving:
Calories: 306
Fat: 5.8g
Carbs: 52.2g
Fiber: 8.8g
Protein: 11.6g

- 300g millet, soaked overnight and rinsed
- 300g can red kidney beans, rinsed and drained
- 1 tbsp basil, fresh or dried   • 1 tbsp fresh parsley, fresh or dried
- 1 tbsp fresh rosemary, fresh or dried
- 2 garlic cloves   • 2 spring onions
- 100g tortilla chips   • 1 large egg, beaten
- Sea salt and ground black pepper, to taste
- 100g Sugo di Pomodoro (Italian tomato sauce)

1. Insert the crisper plates in both drawers and spray them with cooking oil.
2. In your blender or food processor, mix all the ingredients until a thick and uniform batter is formed. Shape the mixture into 7 patties.
3. Now, spray the patties with nonstick cooking oil and then, place them in the zone 1 and 2 drawers.
4. Select zone 1 and pair it with "AIR FRY" at 190°C for 20 minutes. Select "MATCH" to duplicate settings across both zones. Press the "START / STOP" button.
5. When zone 1 time reaches 10 minutes, turn the patties over and spray them with cooking oil on the other side; then, reinsert the drawers to continue cooking.

Bon appétit!

MEDITERRANEAN HERB CORNBREAD MUFFINS

Serves 9
Prep time: 10 minutes
Cook time: 25 minutes

Per Serving:
Calories: 332
Fat: 15.6g
Carbs: 38.5g
Fiber: 1.8g
Protein: 8.6g

- 100ml olive oil   • 200g sweetcorn kernels
- 2 large eggs   • 100ml milk
- 250ml Greek yoghurt   • 160g plain flour
- 200g cornmeal   • 1 / 2 tsp bicarbonate of soda
- 1 tsp baking powder
- 2 tbsp Mediterranean herb mix
- 2 tbsp Kalamata olives, stoned and sliced
- 60g Parmesan cheese, grated

1. Remove a crisper plate from your Ninja Foodi. Lightly spray silicone muffin cases with cooking oil.
2. Mix the liquid ingredients in a bowl; in a separate bowl, mix the dry ingredients. Add the liquid ingredients to the dry flour mixture; stir to combine and fold in the olives and cheese.
3. Spoon the mixture into the prepared muffin cases.
4. Add muffin cases to both drawers. Select zone 1 and pair it with "BAKE" at 180°C for 25 minutes, until golden brown.
5. Select "MATCH" to duplicate settings across both zones. Press the "START / STOP" button.
6. Let your muffins rest for around 10 minutes before unmoulding and serving. Devour!

OAT BAKE WITH FIGS

Serves 6
Prep time: 10 minutes
Cook time: 20 minutes

Per Serving:
Calories: 432   Fat: 9.1g
Carbs: 75.5g   Fiber: 8g
Protein: 14.6g

- 400g old-fashioned oats
- 2 small eggs, beaten
- 6 dried figs, sliced
- 1 / 2 cup clear Mediterranean honey
- 1 tsp vanilla bean paste
- A pinch of grated nutmeg
- 2 tsp olive oil
- 300ml almond milk
- 1 tsp baking powder
- A pinch of ground cinnamon

1. Brush the inside of two oven-safe baking trays with coconut oil. Thoroughly combine all the ingredients; now, spoon the mixture into the prepared baking trays.
2. Select zone 1 and pair it with "BAKE" at 190°C for 20 minutes. Select "MATCH" to duplicate settings across both zones. Press the "START / STOP" button.
3. When zone 1 time reaches 10 minutes, turn the baking tins and reinsert the drawers to resume cooking.
4. Serve with some extra Mediterranean fruits, if desired. Bon appétit!

GREEK PITA WITH SPICY BEANS

Serves 4
Prep time: 10 minutes
Cook time: 15 minutes

Per Serving:
Calories: 365
Fat: 9.1g
Carbs: 55g
Fiber: 7g
Protein: 15.6g

Pita:
- 40ml warm water
- 1 tsp golden caster sugar
- 20ml olive oil
- 1 / 2 tsp dried yeast
- 150g strong bread flour
- 60ml natural yoghurt

Beans:
- Sea salt and ground black pepper, to taste
- 1 tsp Aleppo pepper
- 1 (425g) red kidney beans
- 1 tsp Mediterranean spice mix
- 4 clove garlic, pressed
- 1 red onion, chopped
- 1 tbsp olive oil

1. Remove crisper plates from your Ninja Foodi. Line the zone 1 drawer with baking paper.
2. Whisk the water with yeast and sugar in a mixing dish; let it stand in a warm place for about 10 minutes to activate the yeast.
3. Add the prepared yeast to the flour; add the oil and yoghurt and mix to combine well. Knead the dough until smooth and satin-like dough forms.
4. Next, shape the dough into a ball and place it in the bowl. Cover and leave the dough in a warm place for about 1 hour, until doubled in size.
5. Divide the dough into 4 balls and flatten them using your hands. Add flatbreads to the zone 1 drawer and brush them with olive oil.
6. In a baking tin, thoroughly combine all ingredients for the beans. Add the baking tin to the zone 2 drawer.
7. Select zone 1 and pair it with "BAKE" at 180°C for 15 minutes. Select zone 2 and pair it with "BAKE" at 185°C for 12 minutes. Select "SYNC" followed by the "START / STOP" button. Work in batches, if needed.
8. When zone 1 time reaches 8 minutes, turn the bread over, spray with olive oil on the other side, and reinsert the drawer to continue cooking.
9. Serve a warm pita with beans and enjoy!

SPICED CHICKPEA PATTIES

Serves 4
Prep time: 10 minutes
Cook time: 20 minutes

Per Serving:
Calories: 325
Fat: 7.1g
Carbs: 57.5g
Fiber: 9.7g
Protein: 12g

- 200g buckwheat, soaked overnight, drained and rinsed
- 1 (400g) can chickpeas, rinsed and drained
- 1 large onion, chopped   • 2 medium garlic cloves, minced
- 100g cracker crumbs
- Sea salt and ground black pepper, to taste
- 1 heaped tsp Aleppo pepper • 1 tsp cumin seeds
- 150ml marinara

1. Insert the crisper plates in both drawers and spray them with cooking oil.
2. In your blender or a food processor, thoroughly combine all the ingredients.
3. Now, shape the mixture into 6 patties and spray them with nonstick cooking oil. Now, arrange them in both drawers.
4. Select zone 1 and pair it with "AIR FRY" at 190°C for 20 minutes. Select "MATCH" to duplicate settings across both zones. Press the "START / STOP" button.
5. When zone 1 time reaches 10 minutes, turn the patties over, spray them with cooking oil on the other side, and reinsert the drawers to continue cooking.
6. Serve warm patties in pita with toppings of choice.

Bon appétit!

QUINOA AND CHICKPEA CAKES

Serves 4
Prep time: 10 minutes
Cook time: 20 minutes

Per Serving:
Calories: 355
Fat: 8.1g
Carbs: 57.5g
Fiber: 9.7g
Protein: 12g

- 200g quinoa, soaked overnight, drained and rinsed
- 1 (400g) can chickpeas, rinsed and drained
- 1 medium leek, chopped   • 2 medium garlic cloves, minced
- 100g breadcrumbs   • Sea salt and ground black pepper, to taste
- 1 heaped tsp Aleppo pepper • 1 tbsp olive oil
- 1 tsp dried basil   • 1 tsp dried oregano
- 150ml tomato paste

1. Insert the crisper plates in both drawers and spray them with cooking oil.
2. In your blender or a food processor, thoroughly combine all the ingredients.
3. Now, shape the mixture into 6 patties and spray them with nonstick cooking oil. Now, arrange them in both drawers.
4. Select zone 1 and pair it with "AIR FRY" at 190°C for 20 minutes. Select "MATCH" to duplicate settings across both zones. Press the "START / STOP" button.
5. When zone 1 time reaches 10 minutes, turn the patties over, spray them with cooking oil on the other side, and reinsert the drawers to continue cooking.
6. Serve warm patties in pita with toppings of choice.

Bon appétit!

WHITEFISH RISOTTO WITH CORN

Serves 5
Prep time: 10 minutes
Cook time: 30 minutes

Per Serving:
Calories: 590
Fat: 34.3g
Carbs: 30.2g
Fiber: 2.4g
Protein: 37.3g

- 800g skinless cod fillets, chopped • 1 small carrot, grated
- 1 shallot, chopped • 2 garlic cloves, crushed or finely chopped
- 300ml bottled clam juice • 1 (400g) can tomatoes, chopped
- 2 tbsp olive oil • 300g cooked rice
- 200g frozen corn, thawed • 100g feta cheese, crumbled
- 1 bay laurel
- 1 thyme sprig, leaves finely chopped
- 1 rosemary sprig, leaves finely chopped

1. In a mixing bowl, thoroughly combine the chicken, vegetables, and vegetable broth. Divide the mixture between two baking tins. Add baking tins to the drawers (without crisper plates).
2. Select zone 1 and pair it with "AIR FRY" at 190°C for 15 minutes. Select "MATCH" to duplicate settings across both zones. Press the "START / STOP" button. At the halfway point, gently stir the mixture and reinsert the drawers to resume cooking.
3. Now, add the other ingredients to the baking tins. Gently stir to combine.
4. Select zone 1 and pair it with "BAKE" at 190°C for 15 minutes. Select "MATCH" to duplicate settings across both zones. Press the "START / STOP" button.

Bon appétit!

GRANOLA FIG BARS

Serves 8
Prep time: 10 minutes
Cook time: 20 minutes

Per Serving:
Calories: 255
Fat: 7.5g
Carbs: 42.2g
Fiber: 5.5g
Protein: 7.7g

- 100g oats
- 50g rye flakes
- 1 large banana, mashed
- 100g clear Mediterranean honey
- 50g coconut oil, room temperature
- 50g raw pepitas
- 50g pistachios, slivered
- 1 tsp vanilla essence
- 1 tsp ground cinnamon
- 100g dried figs, chopped

1. Remove a crisper plate from your Ninja Dual Zone Air Fryer.
2. In a mixing bowl, thoroughly combine all the ingredients, except the figs. Line two roasting tins with baking parchment.
3. Tip the mixture into the prepared tins, pressing down lightly with a spatula. Add roasting tins to both drawers.
4. Select zone 1 and pair it with "BAKE" at 180°C for 20 minutes. Select "MATCH" to duplicate settings across both zones. Press the "START / STOP" button.
5. Add the figs and stir to combine. Bon appétit!

MACARONI AND BEAN CASSEROLE

Serves 8
Prep time: 10 minutes
Cook time: 30 minutes

Per Serving:
Calories: 381
Fat: 7.3g
Carbs: 57.7g
Fiber: 6g
Protein: 17.3g

- 400g macaroni
- 200g canned or cooked red kidney beans, rinsed and drained
- 200g canned or cooked Cannellini beans, rinsed and drained
- 200ml chicken stock   • 220ml tomato sauce
- Sea salt and ground black pepper, to taste
- 1 large bell pepper, deseeded and sliced
- 2 celery sticks, finely chopped
- 1 onion, sliced   • 2 garlic cloves, chopped
- 160g Parmesan cheese, preferably freshly grated
- 60g breadcrumbs

1. Remove crisper plates from your Ninja Dual Zone Air Fryer.
2. Cook your macaroni following pack instructions; drain and reserve.
3. Thoroughly combine the beans, stock, tomato sauce, salt, black pepper, and vegetables in a large bowl; gently stir to combine.
4. Spoon the mixture into two lightly greased baking trays. Add the baking trays to the drawers.
5. Select zone 1 and pair it with "BAKE" at 180°C for 30 minutes. Select "MATCH" followed by the "START / STOP" button.
6. At the halfway point, gently stir the ingredients. Top with cheese and breadcrumbs; reinsert the drawers to resume cooking.

Bon appétit!

MARINARA LENTIL CASSEROLE

Serves 6
Prep time: 10 minutes
Cook time: 21 minutes

Per Serving:
Calories: 410
Fat: 16.5g
Carbs: 41.8g
Fiber: 16g
Protein: 24.3g

- 2 tbsp olive oil   • 1 red onion, chopped
- 2 medium carrots, thinly sliced   • 200ml marinara sauce
- 1 small celery stalk, peeled and thinly sliced
- 2 garlic cloves, finely chopped   • 1 bay leaf
- 1 thyme sprig, leaves picked and chopped
- 1kg canned or cooked red lentils, rinsed and drained
- 200g Asiago cheese, preferably freshly grated

1. Heat 1 tablespoon of olive oil in a pan over medium-high heat. Sauté the onion and vegetables for about 3 minutes, until they're just tender.
2. Then, sauté the garlic, thyme, and bay leaf for about 30 seconds, until they are aromatic.
3. Brush the inside of two baking tins with the remaining 1 tablespoon of olive oil. Add the sauteed mixture along with the spices, beans, marinara, and parsley to the baking tins; gently stir to combine and lower them into the drawers.
4. Select zone 1 and pair it with "AIR FRY" at 180°C for 18 minutes. Select "MATCH" to duplicate the setting across both zones. Press the "START / STOP" button.
5. When zone 1 time reaches 11 minutes, top your casseroles with cheese and reinsert the drawers to continue cooking.
6. Serve warm and enjoy!

MEDITRRANEAN COUSCOUS

Serves 4
Prep time: 5 minutes
Cook time: 24 minutes

Per Serving:
Calories: 254
Fat: 4.1g
Carbs: 45.2g
Fiber: 4.1g
Protein: 9.2g

- 250g cremini mushrooms, sliced
- 1 medium bell pepper, whole
- 1 tbsp olive oil
- 1 tbsp fresh sage
- 1 tbsp fresh rosemary
- Sea salt and ground black pepper, to taste
- 200g couscous
- 200ml water
- 1 medium courgette, quartered
- 1 medium onion, halved
- 1 tbsp fresh parsley

1. Toss your vegetables with olive oil and spices; lower the courgette and mushrooms into the zone 1 drawer and peppers and onions into the zone 2 drawer.
2. Select zone 1 and pair it with "AIR FRY" at 190°C for 16 minutes. Select zone 2 and pair it with "AIR FRY" at 200°C for 10 minutes. Select "SYNC" followed by the "START / STOP" button. Your vegetables will still be a bit crispy.
3. Meanwhile, cook your couscous in boiling water for about 10 minutes. Add your couscous to two lightly oiled casserole dishes.
4. Add the other ingredients and gently stir to combine. Next, bake it at 190°C for about 8 minutes using the "BAKE" function.

Enjoy!

PARMESAN MARINARA BEANS

Serves 8
Prep time: 10 minutes
Cook time: 25 minutes

Per Serving:
Calories: 333
Fat: 9.3g
Carbs: 41.7g
Fiber: 12.6g
Protein: 19.3g

- 2 tsp olive oil
- 2 garlic cloves, finely chopped
- 2 medium Italian peppers, deseeded and sliced
- 1 / 2 tsp cumin seeds
- 1kg cooked Cannellini beans, drained and rinsed
- 2 tbsp fresh Italian parsley leaves, chopped
- 100ml Mediterranean red cooking wine
- 1 red onion, chopped
- 1 bay leaf
- 200ml marinara
- 200g Parmesan cheese, grated

1. Heat 1 teaspoon of olive oil in a pan over medium-high heat. Sauté the onion and peppers for about 3 minutes, until they're just tender.
2. Then, sauté the garlic, bay leaf, and cumin for about 30 seconds, until fragrant.
3. Brush the inside of two baking tins with the remaining 1 teaspoon of olive oil. Add the sauteed mixture along with the spices, beans, marinara, and parsley to the baking tins; gently stir to combine and lower them into the drawers.
4. Select zone 1 and pair it with "AIR FRY" at 180°C for 20 minutes. Select "MATCH" to duplicate the setting across both zones. Press the "START / STOP" button.
5. When zone 1 time reaches 10 minutes, add the wine and gently stir your beans; top them with cheese and reinsert the drawers to continue cooking.

Devour!

QUINOA PUDDING WITH PISTACHIOS AND FIGS

Serves 5
Prep time: 10 minutes
Cook time: 15 minutes

Per Serving:
Calories: 581
Fat: 21.9g
Carbs: 79.2g
Fiber: 9.4g
Protein: 21.3g

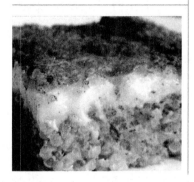

- 2 tsp olive oil, melted
- 350g quinoa, soaked overnight and rinsed
- 100g dried figs, chopped
- 100g pistachios, chopped
- 1 large banana, peeled and mashed
- 1 litre almond milk
- 1 vanilla bean, split
- 1 cinnamon stick

1. Brush the inside of two oven-safe baking tins with coconut oil.
2. Mix the quinoa with the other ingredients and spoon the mixture into the baking trays. Add the baking trays to the drawers.
3. Select zone 1 and pair it with "BAKE" at 180°C for 15 minutes. Select "MATCH" to duplicate settings across both zones. Press the "START / STOP" button.
4. When zone 1 time reaches 7 minutes, rotate both baking tins and reinsert the drawers to continue cooking.
5. Bon appétit!

BAKLAVA OATMEAL

Serves 5
Prep time: 10 minutes
Cook time: 20 minutes

Per Serving:
Calories: 469
Fat: 11.1g
Carbs: 80.1g
Fiber: 8g
Protein: 15.6g

- 350g old-fashioned oats
- 2 tsp coconut oil
- 400ml whole milk
- 1 / 2 cup clear Mediterranean honey
- A pinch of ground cinnamon
- 1 tsp vanilla bean paste
- A pinch of grated nutmeg
- 1 tbsp lemon zest finely grated
- 3 tbsp pistachios, roughly chopped

1. Brush the inside of two oven-safe baking trays with coconut oil. Thoroughly combine all the ingredients; now, spoon the mixture into the prepared baking trays.
2. Select zone 1 and pair it with "BAKE" at 190°C for 20 minutes. Select "MATCH" to duplicate settings across both zones. Press the "START / STOP" button.
3. When zone 1 time reaches 10 minutes, turn the baking tins and reinsert the drawers to resume cooking.
Devour!

GREEK-STYLE SAVOURY MUFFINS

Serves 9
Prep time: 10 minutes
Cook time: 25 minutes

Per Serving:
Calories: 330
Fat: 17g
Carbs: 34.5g
Fiber: 2.1g
Protein: 8.8g

- 2 large eggs
- 200ml Greek yoghurt
- 100ml sparkling water
- 100ml olive oil
- 200g cornmeal
- 150g plain flour
- 1 / 2 tsp bicarbonate of soda
- 1 tsp baking powder
- 1 tbsp Italian herb mix
- 4 sun-dried tomatoes in oil, chopped
- 100g feta cheese, grated

1. Remove a crisper plate from your Ninja Foodi. Lightly spray silicone muffin cases with cooking oil.
2. Mix the liquid ingredients in a bowl; in a separate bowl, mix the dry ingredients. Add the liquid ingredients to the dry flour mixture; stir to combine and fold in the tomatoes and cheese.
3. Spoon the mixture into the prepared muffin cases.
4. Add muffin cases to both drawers. Select zone 1 and pair it with "BAKE" at 180°C for 25 minutes, until golden brown.
5. Select "MATCH" to duplicate settings across both zones. Press the "START / STOP" button.
6. Let your muffins rest for around 10 minutes before unmoulding and serving. Devour!

CHAPTER 6
APPETIZERS
&
LIGHT BITES

MEDITERRANEAN HERB POTATOES

Serves 6
Prep time: 10 minutes
Cook time: 20 minutes

Per Serving:
Calories: 153
Fat: 2.7g
Carbs: 30.1g
Fiber: 3.6g
Protein: 5g

- 1kg potatoes, peeled and cut into wedges
- 1 tbsp fresh rosemary leaves, chopped
- 1 tbsp fresh parsley leaves, chopped
- 1 tbsp fresh basil leaves, chopped
- 1 tbsp olive oil
- 1 tbsp fresh lemon juice
- Sea salt and ground black pepper, to taste

1. Toss the potatoes with the other ingredients. Place the potatoes in both drawers.
2. Select zone 1 and pair it with "ROAST" at 200°C for 20 minutes. Select "MATCH" followed by the "START / STOP" button.
3. Cook the potatoes until slightly charred and enjoy!

STICKY ROOT VEGS

Serves 5
Prep time: 10 minutes
Cook time: 20 minutes

Per Serving:
Calories: 133
Fat: 5.7g
Carbs: 20g
Fiber: 3.9g
Protein: 1.9g

- 300g celery root, peeled, cut into sticks
- 300g carrots, cut into sticks
- 100g parsnips, cut into sticks
- 2 tbsp olive oil
- 2 tbsp red wine vinegar
- 1 tsp Aleppo pepper
- 1 tbsp Mediterranean herb mix
- Sea salt and black pepper, to taste
- 2 tbsp clear Mediterranean honey

1. Tip the vegetables into two roasting tins and toss them with the other ingredients.
2. Select zone 1 and pair it with "ROAST" at 180°C for 20 minutes. Select "MATCH" to duplicate settings across both zones. Press the "START / STOP" button.
3. When zone 1 time reaches 10 minutes, toss the vegetables with maple syrup and reinsert the drawers to continue cooking.

Bon appétit!

GLAZED BRUSSELS SPROUTS

Serves 6
Prep time: 10 minutes
Cook time: 13 minutes

Per Serving:
Calories: 159
Fat: 5.5g
Carbs: 23.8g
Fiber: 6.7g
Protein: 6.1g

- 1kg Brussels sprouts, whole
- 2 tbsp polenta
- 2 tbsp olive oil
- 2 tbsp red wine vinegar
- 2 tbsp Mediterranean honey
- Sea salt and black pepper, to taste

1. Tip Brussels sprouts into two roasting tins and toss them with the other ingredients.
2. Select zone 1 and pair it with "ROAST" at 190°C for 13 minutes. Select "MATCH" to duplicate settings across both zones. Press the "START / STOP" button.
3. When zone 1 time reaches 6 minutes, shake the basket and reinsert the drawers to continue cooking.

Bon appétit!

PARMESAN BROCCOLI BITES

Serves 5
Prep time: 10 minutes
Cook time: 15 minutes

Per Serving:
Calories: 229
Fat: 9.1g
Carbs: 28.8g
Fiber: 5.7g
Protein: 11.7g

- 1kg broccoli florets
- 100ml marinara sauce
- 20ml port wine
- 1 tbsp Mediterranean clear honey
- 1 tbsp olive oil
- 1 tsp dried oregano
- 1 tsp dried basil
- 1 tbsp dried parsley flakes
- 1 / 4 tsp ground bay laurel
- Sea salt and ground black pepper, to taste
- 100g parmesan cheese, grated

1. Insert the crisper plates in both drawers and spray them with cooking oil.
2. Toss broccoli florets with the other ingredients, except the cheese. Arrange broccoli florets on the prepared crisper plates.
3. Select zone 1 and pair it with "ROAST" at 180°C for 15 minutes. Select "MATCH" to duplicate settings across both zones. Press the "START / STOP" button.
4. When zone 1 time reaches 10 minutes, toss the broccoli florets with cheese and reinsert the drawers to continue cooking.

Bon appétit!

GREEN BEAN CHIPS

Serves 5
Prep time: 10 minutes
Cook time: 12 minutes

Per Serving:
Calories: 88
Fat: 3.1g
Carbs: 13.8g
Fiber: 5.5g
Protein: 3.7g

- 1 kg green beans, trimmed
- 1 tbsp olive oil, divided
- 1 tsp dried oregano
- 1 tsp garlic granules
- 1 tsp Aleppo pepper
- Sea salt and black pepper, to taste

1. Toss green beans with olive oil and spices. Add green beans to both drawers (with a crisper plate inserted).
2. Select zone 1 and pair it with "AIR FRY" at 200°C for 12 minutes. Select "MATCH" followed by the "START / STOP" button.
3. When zone 1 time reaches 5 minutes, shake the drawers and toss green beans with Parmesan cheese. Reinsert the drawers to continue cooking.
4. Devour!

CHEESY STUFFED MUSHROOMS

Serves 6
Prep time: 10 minutes
Cook time: 14 minutes

Per Serving:
Calories: 88
Fat: 3.1g
Carbs: 13.8g
Fiber: 5.5g
Protein: 3.7g

- 600g button mushrooms, cleaned and stems removed
- 2 large eggs
- Sea salt and ground black pepper, to taste
- 1 tsp dried parsley flakes
- 1 tsp garlic granules
- 1 tsp dried oregano
- 100g plain flour
- 50g tortilla chips, crushed
- 50g Provolone cheese, grated
- 1 tbsp olive oil

1. Insert crisper plates in both drawers. Spray crisper plates with nonstick cooking oil.
2. Pat the mushrooms dry using tea (paper) towels.
3. Create the breading station: Beat the eggs until pale and frothy. In a separate shallow dish, mix the spices and flour. In a third shallow dish, thoroughly combine the crushed tortilla chips with cheese and olive oil.
4. Dip the mushrooms in the egg, then, dust your mushrooms with the flour mixture. Roll them over the tortilla chip mixture, pressing to adhere.
5. Arrange the prepared mushrooms on the crisper plates.
6. Select zone 1 and pair it with "AIR FRY" at 190°C for 14 minutes. Select "MATCH" to duplicate settings across both zones. Press the "START / STOP" button.
7. When zone 1 time reaches 7 minutes, turn the mushrooms over using silicone-tipped tongs. Reinsert the drawers to continue cooking. Enjoy!

CHEESE ASPARAGUS BITES

Serves 5
Prep time: 10 minutes
Cook time: 10 minutes

Per Serving:
Calories: 134
Fat: 3.6g
Carbs: 25.4g
Fiber: 6.2g
Protein: 4.2g

- 1kg asparagus spears, trimmed
- 1 tsp onion powder
- 1 tsp garlic granules
- 1 / 2 tsp dried basil
- 1 / 2 tsp dried dill weed
- Sea salt and ground black pepper, to taste
- 1 tbsp olive oil
- 100g Parmesan cheese, grated

1. Pat dry the asparagus with tea towels and cut off the tips. Toss the asparagus pieces with the other ingredients, except cheese.
2. Add the asparagus spears to both drawers.
3. Select zone 1 and pair it with "AIR FRY" at 200°C for 10 minutes. Select "MATCH" followed by the "START / STOP" button.
4. At the halfway point, top your asparagus with the cheese; reinsert the drawers to resume cooking.

Devour!

EASY CRAB STICKS

Serves 5
Prep time: 10 minutes
Cook time: 15 minutes

Per Serving:
Calories: 340
Fat: 13.6g
Carbs: 17.3g
Fiber: 0.2g
Protein: 0.8g

- 800g crab sticks, cut into bite-sized pieces
- 100g cornmeal
- 2 tbsp fresh lemon juice
- 2 tsp olive oil
- 1 tsp garlic, crushed
- 1 tbsp fresh parsley, chopped
- 1 tbsp fresh basil, chopped

1. Insert crisper plates in both drawers and spray them with cooking oil.
2. Toss crab sticks with the other ingredients and place them on crisper plates.
3. Select zone 1 and pair it with "AIR FRY" at 160°C for 15 minutes. Select "MATCH" to duplicate settings across both zones. Press the "START / STOP" button.
4. Shake the drawers halfway through the cooking time to ensure even cooking.

Devour!

VEGETABLE KABOBS

Serves 5
Prep time: 10 minutes
Cook time: 18 minutes

Per Serving:
Calories: 340
Fat: 13.6g
Carbs: 17.3g
Fiber: 0.2g
Protein: 0.8g

- 4 bell peppers, deseeded and sliced
- 8 small button mushrooms, whole
- 1 medium aubergine, cut into thick slices
- 1 medium courgette, cut into thick slices
- 4 small shallots, quartered
- 100g cherry tomatoes
- 1 tbsp Italian herb mix
- Sea salt and ground black pepper, to taste
- 1 tbsp olive oil
- 1 tsp balsamic vinegar

1. Toss all the ingredients until vegetables are well coated on all sides.
2. Alternately thread the vegetables onto the skewers until you run out of the ingredients.
3. Then, add the vegetable kabobs to the zone 1 and 2 drawers.
4. Select zone 1 and pair it with "ROAST" at 180°C for 18 minutes. Select "MATCH" followed by the "START / STOP" button.
5. At the halfway point, turn the kabobs over and reinsert the drawers to resume cooking.

Bon appétit!

MEDITERRANEAN GRILLED STREET CORN

Serves 4
Prep time: 10 minutes
Cook time: 15 minutes

Per Serving:
Calories: 243
Fat: 10.3g
Carbs: 34.3g
Fiber: 4.2g
Protein: 9.7g

- 4 ears corn on the cob, halved
- 2 tsp olive oil
- 4 tbsp Greek yoghurt, plain
- 4 tbsp feta cheese, crumbled
- 2 sun-dried tomatoes, chopped
- 1 tbsp fresh parsley flakes
- 2 tbsp fresh oregano, chopped
- 1 tbsp fresh basil, chopped
- Flaky sea salt and ground black pepper, to taste

1. In a small mixing bowl, thoroughly combine the olive oil, Greek yoghurt, feta cheese, sun-dried tomatoes, herbs, salt, and black pepper.
2. Cut 8 pieces of tin foil and place 1 / 2 of the cob on each piece. Transfer the packets to the cooking basket.
3. Select zone 1 and pair it with "BAKE" at 190°C for 15 minutes. Select "MATCH" followed by the "START / STOP" button.
4. At the halfway point, top your corn with the feta herb mixture; reinsert the drawer to continue cooking.
5. Serve warm and enjoy!

MARINARA CAULIFLOWER BITES

Serves 4
Prep time: 10 minutes
Cook time: 20 minutes

Per Serving:
Calories: 143
Fat: 4.3g
Carbs: 23.3g
Fiber: 5.4g
Protein: 5.2g

- 1kg cauliflower florets
- 100ml marinara sauce
- 1 tbsp olive oil
- Sea salt and ground black pepper, to taste

1. Insert the crisper plates in both drawers and spray them with cooking oil.
2. Toss cauliflower florets with the other ingredients. Arrange cauliflower florets on the prepared crisper plates.
3. Select zone 1 and pair it with "ROAST" at 190°C for 20 minutes. Select "MATCH" to duplicate settings across both zones. Press the "START / STOP" button.

Bon appétit!

BEAN AND BARLEY CROQUETTES

Serves 6
Prep time: 10 minutes
Cook time: 20 minutes

Per Serving:
Calories: 263
Fat: 2.3g
Carbs: 53.3g
Fiber: 11.4g
Protein: 10.5g

- 400g canned or cooked cannellini beans, drained and rinsed
- 400g barley, cooked
- 1 small aubergine, chopped
- 1 medium courgette, peeled
- 1 medium leek
- 2 garlic cloves, peeled
- 4 tbsp marinara sauce
- 100g instant oats

1. Insert the crisper plates in both drawers and spray them with cooking oil.
2. Blend all the ingredients in your food processor. Shape the mixture into 8 balls and lower them into both drawers.
3. Select zone 1 and pair it with "AIR FRY" at 185°C for 20 minutes. Select "MATCH" to duplicate settings across both zones. Press the "START / STOP" button.
4. When zone 1 time reaches 10 minutes, turn the croquettes over and reinsert the drawers to resume cooking.
5. Serve warm croquettes with the sauce for dipping and enjoy!

SPICY FALAFEL

Serves 9
Prep time: 10 minutes
Cook time: 22 minutes

Per Serving:
Calories: 181
Fat: 3.9g
Carbs: 28.8g
Fiber: 8g
Protein: 8.5g

- 800g canned or cooked chickpeas, drained and rinsed
- 1 large carrot, peeled
- 1 large red onion
- 2 garlic cloves, peeled
- 1 medium bell pepper, deseeded
- 4 tbsp marinara sauce
- Sea salt and ground black pepper, to taste
- 1 tbsp Mediterranean spice mix
- 1 tbsp olive oil

1. Insert the crisper plates in both drawers and spray them with cooking oil.
2. Mix all the ingredients in your food processor or a high-speed blender. Shape the mixture into 9 balls and lower them into both drawers.
3. Select zone 1 and pair it with "AIR FRY" at 185°C for 22 minutes. Select "MATCH" to duplicate settings across both zones. Press the "START / STOP" button.
4. When zone 1 time reaches 12 minutes, turn the falafel balls over and reinsert the drawers to continue cooking.
5. Sere warm falafel balls with toothpicks and enjoy!

GREEK CHICKEN NUGGETS

Serves 6
Prep time: 10 minutes
Cook time: 18 minutes

Per Serving:
Calories: 373
Fat: 16.4g
Carbs: 21.8g
Fiber: 2.3g
Protein: 33.5g

- 800g chicken breast, cut into bite-sized pieces
- 160ml natural Greek yoghurt
- 2 tbsp Mediterranean red wine
- 1 tbsp stone ground mustard
- Sea salt and ground black pepper, to taste
- 1 tsp Greek oregano
- 160g cornflakes, crushed
- 1 tbsp olive oil

1. Toss the chicken pieces with Greek yoghurt, Mediterranean red wine, mustard, salt, black pepper, and oregano in a ceramic bowl. Leave it to marinate in your fridge for about 3 hours.
2. Discard the marinade and press each piece of the marinated chicken onto the crushed cornflakes, pressing to adhere. Brush the chicken pieces with olive oil and arrange them in both drawers.
3. Select zone 1 and pair it with "AIR FRY" at 200°C for 18 minutes. Select "MATCH" to duplicate settings across both zones. Press the "START / STOP" button.
4. When zone 1 time reaches 9 minutes, shake the basket to ensure even cooking. Reinsert the drawers to continue cooking.
Enjoy!

BEAN AND BARLEY CROQUETTES

Serves 6
Prep time: 10 minutes
Cook time: 20 minutes

Per Serving:
Calories: 366
Fat: 8.3g
Carbs: 58.3g
Fiber: 10.2g
Protein: 15.2g

- 400g canned or cooked red lentils, drained and rinsed
- 300g quinoa, soaked overnight
- 1 medium Italian pepper, seeded and chopped
- 1 medium courgette, peeled
- 1 large red onion
- 2 garlic cloves, peeled
- 4 tbsp marinara sauce
- 100g breadcrumbs
- 2 tbsp olive oil

1. Insert the crisper plates in both drawers and spray them with cooking oil.
2. Blend all the ingredients in your food processor. Shape the mixture into 12 small balls and lower them into both drawers.
3. Select zone 1 and pair it with "AIR FRY" at 185°C for 20 minutes. Select "MATCH" to duplicate settings across both zones. Press the "START / STOP" button.
4. When zone 1 time reaches 10 minutes, turn the croquettes over and reinsert the drawers to resume cooking.

Bon appétit!

CHAPTER 7
VEGAN &
VEGETARIAN

BROCCOLI LENTIL CAKES

Serves 5
Prep time: 10 minutes
Cook time: 20 minutes

Per Serving:
Calories: 256
Fat: 4.9g
Carbs: 41.3g
Fiber: 12g
Protein: 14.2g

- 600g small broccoli florets
- 1 (400g) cans of red lentils, rinsed drained and mashed
- 1 medium onion, peeled
- 2 garlic cloves, peeled
- 100g instant oats
- 1 / 2 tsp ground leaf
- 1 / 2 tsp ground cumin
- Sea salt and ground black pepper, to taste
- 1 tbsp olive oil

1. Insert the crisper plates in both drawers and spray them with cooking oil.
2. Add all the ingredients to a bowl of your food processor. Blend the ingredients until everything is well incorporated.
3. Shape the mixture into equal patties and arrange them on the crisper plates.
4. Select zone 1 and pair it with "AIR FRY" at 180°C for 20 minutes. Select "MATCH" to duplicate settings across both zones. Press the "START / STOP" button.
5. When zone 1 time reaches 10 minutes, turn the cakes over and spray them with cooking oil on the other side; reinsert the drawers to continue cooking.

Bon appétit!

ROASTED COURGETTE WITH TOFU

Serves 5
Prep time: 10 minutes
Cook time: 12 minutes

Per Serving:
Calories: 156
Fat: 9g
Carbs: 8.7g
Fiber: 2.2g
Protein: 14g

- 500g courgette, sliced
- 500g tofu, pressed and sliced
- 1 tsp garlic granules
- 1 / 2 tsp cumin powder
- 2 tsp olive oil
- 100ml marinara sauce

1. Toss courgette and tofu with spices, olive oil, and sauce.
2. Arrange bell peppers in the zone 1 drawer and tofu in the zone 2 drawer.
3. Select zone 1 and pair it with "ROAST" at 190°C for 12 minutes. Select zone 2 and pair it with "ROAST" at 180°C for 10 minutes. Select "SYNC" followed by the "START / STOP" button.
4. When zone 1 time reaches 6 minutes, toss the drawer to ensure even cooking; reinsert the drawer to resume cooking.
5. When zone 2 time reaches 5 minutes, shake the drawer and reinsert it to resume cooking.

Bon appétit!

BUCKWHEAT AND CARROT PATTIES

Serves 4
Prep time: 10 minutes
Cook time: 20 minutes

Per Serving:
Calories: 248
Fat: 5.6g
Carbs: 45.3g
Fiber: 8.2g
Protein: 9.6g

• 200g buckwheat, soaked overnight and rinsed
• 500g cauliflower florets
• 1 shallot, peeled
• 2 garlic cloves, peeled
• 1 tsp Mediterranean spices mix
• Sea salt and ground black pepper, to taste
• 1 tbsp olive oil

1. Insert the crisper plates in both drawers and spray them with cooking oil.
2. Add all the ingredients to a bowl of your food processor. Blend the ingredients until everything is well incorporated.
3. Shape the mixture into equal patties and arrange them on the crisper plates.
4. Select zone 1 and pair it with "AIR FRY" at 180°C for 20 minutes. Select "MATCH" to duplicate settings across both zones. Press the "START / STOP" button.
5. When zone 1 time reaches 10 minutes, turn your burgers over and spray them with cooking oil on the other side; reinsert the drawers to resume cooking.

Bon appétit!

MUSHROOM AND BEAN STUFFED TOMATOES

Serves 4
Prep time: 10 minutes
Cook time: 12 minutes

Per Serving:
Calories: 384
Fat: 18.6g
Carbs: 34.8g
Fiber: 7.4g
Protein: 23.4g

• 4 large tomatoes (beefsteak or heirloom)
• 400g cremini mushrooms, chopped
• 200g canned red kidney beans, drained and rinsed
• 100g green olives, stoned and chopped
• 1 large red onion, chopped
• Sea salt and cracked black pepper, to taste
• 2 garlic cloves, minced
• 200g parmesan cheese, preferably freshly grated

1. Slice the tops off the tomatoes. Then, scoop out the seeds and pulp from them, discarding the central cores.
2. In a bowl, mix the mushrooms, beans, olives, onion, salt, black pepper, and garlic. Divide the stuffing mixture between the prepared tomatoes.
3. Lower the tomatoes into both drawers.
4. Select zone 1 and pair it with "AIR FRY" at 190°C for 12 minutes. Select "MATCH" followed by the "START / STOP" button.
5. When zone 1 time reaches 6 minutes, top them with cheese and continue to cook for a further 6 minutes, until cooked through.

TWISTED RED BEETROOT FALAFEL

Serves 5
Prep time: 10 minutes
Cook time: 1 hour 5 minutes

Per Serving:
Calories: 264
Fat: 7.6g
Carbs: 40.8g
Fiber: 11.4g
Protein: 10.6g

- 500g raw small beetroots, peeled and trimmed
- 500g canned or boiled chickpeas, drained and rinsed
- 1 large carrot, peeled • 1 large courgette, peeled
- 1 large red onion • 2 garlic cloves, peeled
- 1 tsp Aleppo pepper • 4 tbsp tomato passata
- 1 tbsp olive oil • 1 tbsp tahini

1. Insert the crisper plates in both drawers and spray them with cooking oil.
2. Add beetroots to the cooking basket; now, select zone 1 and pair it with "AIR FRY" at 200°C for 45 minutes. Select "MATCH" to duplicate settings across both zones. Press the "START / STOP" button.
3. When the beets are cool enough to handle, add them to your food processor or a high-speed blender. Add the other ingredients and mix until everything is well incorporated.
4. Shape the mixture into 10-12 balls and lower them into both drawers.
5. Select zone 1 and pair it with "AIR FRY" at 185°C for 20 minutes. Select "MATCH" to duplicate settings across both zones. Press the "START / STOP" button.
6. When zone 1 time reaches 10 minutes, shake the cooking basket and reinsert the drawers to continue cooking.
7. Serve warm falafel balls in pita bread and enjoy!

TOFU AND HUMMUS STUFFED MUSHROOMS

Serves 6
Prep time: 10 minutes
Cook time: 15 minutes

Per Serving:
Calories: 114
Fat: 4.6g
Carbs: 11.4g
Fiber: 2.6g
Protein: 8.6g

- 6 Portobello mushrooms
- 400g tofu, pressed and crumbled
- 100g hummus
- 1 red onion, chopped
- 2 garlic cloves, minced
- 2 tbsp fresh parsley leaves, chopped
- 1 tsp Aleppo pepper
- Sea salt and ground black pepper, to taste

1. Pat the mushrooms dry with paper towels and remove the stems; chop the stems and reserve.
2. Mix the mushroom stems with the other ingredients. Stir to combine and divide the filling between portobello mushrooms.
3. Place the stuffed mushrooms in both drawers and brush them with olive oil.
4. Select zone 1 and pair it with "ROAST" at 180°C for 15 minutes. Select "MATCH" followed by the "START / STOP" button.
5. Bon appétit!

VEGAN FRIED WINGS

Serves 5
Prep time: 10 minutes
Cook time: 20 minutes

Per Serving:
Calories: 222
Fat: 12.8g
Carbs: 22.3g
Fiber: 5.8g
Protein: 8.9g

- 1kg cauliflower florets
- 100ml marinara sauce
- 1 tsp Aleppo pepper
- 2 tbsp olive oil
- 2 tbsp nutritional yeast
- 4 tbsp tahini sauce
- 1 tbsp fresh lemon juice
- 4 tbsp plain flour
- 1 tbsp Greek spice mix for poultry
- Sea salt and ground black pepper, to taste

1. Insert the crisper plates in both drawers and spray them with cooking oil. Pat the cauliflower florets dy with kitchen (tea) towels.
2. Mix the other ingredients in a bowl. Coat the prepared cauliflower florets with the flour mixture.
3. Arrange cauliflower florets on the prepared crisper plates.
4. Select zone 1 and pair it with "ROAST" at 190°C for 20 minutes. Select "MATCH" to duplicate settings across both zones. Press the "START / STOP" button.

Bon appétit!

VEGAN LENTIL BURGERS

Serves 5
Prep time: 10 minutes
Cook time: 20 minutes

Per Serving:
Calories: 323
Fat: 11.4g
Carbs: 43g
Fiber: 12.2g
Protein: 15.5g

- 1 (400g) can of red lentils, rinsed drained and mashed
- 600g small cauliflower flowers
- 100g instant oats
- 1 medium carrot, diced
- 1 medium celeriac, diced
- 1 medium leek
- 2 garlic cloves, peeled
- 4 tbsp flax seed meal
- 1 tsp ground cumin
- Sea salt and ground black pepper, to taste
- 2 tbsp olive oil

1. Insert the crisper plates in both drawers and spray them with cooking oil.
2. Add all the ingredients to a bowl of your food processor. Blend the ingredients until everything is well incorporated.
3. Shape the mixture into burger patties and place them on the crisper plates.
4. Select zone 1 and pair it with "AIR FRY" at 180°C for 20 minutes. Select "MATCH" to duplicate settings across both zones. Press the "START / STOP" button.
5. When zone 1 time reaches 10 minutes, turn the patties over and spray them with cooking oil on the other side; reinsert the drawers to continue cooking.

Bon appétit!

LAVENDER ESPRESSO PANCAKES

Serves 6
Prep time: 10 minutes
Cook time: 20 minutes

Per Serving:
Calories: 337
Fat: 7.2g
Carbs: 54.4g
Fiber: 7.4g
Protein: 14.5g

- 400g old-fashioned rolled oats
- 2 eggs
- 200ml almond milk
- 1 tsp vanilla extract
- 1 tsp pure maple syrup
- 2 tsp baking powder
- 1 tsp ground cinnamon
- 1 tbsp lavender
- A pinch of sea salt
- Olive oil, for cooking
- 400g unsweetened applesauce

1. Begin by preheating your Ninja Dual Zone Air Fryer to 180°C. Now, brush two muffin tins with nonstick cooking spray.
2. In your food processor, mix all the ingredients until everything is well incorporated.
3. Spoon the batter into the prepared muffin tins. Lower one muffin tin into each drawer.
4. Select zone 1 and pair it with "BAKE" at 180°C for 20 minutes. Select "MATCH" followed by the "START / STOP" button.
5. Transfer your pancakes to a cooling rack; let it stand for about 10 minutes before unmolding and serving.

Bon appétit!

GREEK STUFFED PEPPERS

Serves 6
Prep time: 10 minutes
Cook time: 23 minutes

Per Serving:
Calories: 254
Fat: 12.6g
Carbs: 28g
Fiber: 3.5g
Protein: 11.4g

- 6 bell peppers, deveined
- 1 small courgette, grated
- 250g jar antipasti marinated mushrooms
- 50g Kalamata olives, pitted, chopped
- 100g quinoa, soaked overnight
- 200g halloumi cheese, crumbled
- 2 tsp chopped fresh parsley
- 1 tbsp dried oregano
- Sea salt and ground black pepper, to taste
- 1 tbsp olive oil

1. Brush the peppers with olive oil and place them in both drawers.
2. Select zone 1 and pair it with "ROAST" at 180°C for 10 minutes. Select "MATCH" to duplicate settings across both zones. Press the "START / STOP" button.
3. In a mixing bowl, thoroughly combine the other ingredients. Divide the mixture between bell peppers and arrange the peppers in baking tins.
4. Place the tins in the cooking basket of your Ninja Foodi.
5. Select zone 1 and pair it with "BAKE" at 185°C for 13 minutes. Select "MATCH" to duplicate settings across both zones. Press the "START / STOP" button.

Bon appétit!

VEGAN CROQUETTES WITH MEDITERRANEAN HERBS

Serves 6
Prep time: 10 minutes
Cook time: 20 minutes

Per Serving:
Calories: 389
Fat: 5.8g
Carbs: 70.3g
Fiber: 16.4g
Protein: 18.5g

• 2 (400g) cans Italian butterbeans, drained and rinsed
• 400g barley, cooked   • 1 medium aubergine, chopped
• 1 large red onion, peeled and quartered
• 1 Italian pepper, deseeded and sliced
• 2 garlic cloves, peeled   • 4 tbsp marinara sauce
• 2 tbsp fresh parsley   • 2 tbsp fresh basil
• 100g instant oats   • 2 tbsp chia seeds
• 2 tsp olive oil

1. Insert the crisper plates in both drawers and spray them with cooking oil.
2. Blend all the ingredients in your food processor. Let the mixture stand for 1 hour in your fridge; this will help you to shape them easier.
3. Shape the mixture into equal balls and lower them into both drawers.
4. Select zone 1 and pair it with "AIR FRY" at 185°C for 20 minutes. Select "MATCH" to duplicate settings across both zones. Press the "START / STOP" button.
5. When zone 1 time reaches 10 minutes, shake the basket to ensure even browning; reinsert the drawers to resume cooking.
6. Serve warm croquettes in pita bread and enjoy!

BROCCOLI CARROT FRITTERS

Serves 6
Prep time: 10 minutes
Cook time: 20 minutes

Per Serving:
Calories: 381
Fat: 16.6g
Carbs: 39.4g
Fiber: 7.7g
Protein: 20.8g

• 800g broccoli, coarsely grated
• 200g carrots, grated
• 2 large eggs, beaten
• 200g oat flour
• 1 tsp baking powder
• 1 tsp bicarbonate of soda
• 1 medium onion, sliced
• 1 tbsp olive oil
• 1 tbsp Italian herb mix
• Sea salt and black pepper to taste
• 200g parmesan cheese, grated

1. Line the bottom of the crisper plates with baking parchment.
2. Mix the ingredients until everything is well incorporated.
3. Shape the mixture into patties, flattening them down with the back of a spoon into disc shapes.
4. Place the patties on crisper plates. Select zone 1 and pair it with "AIR FRY" at 180°C for 20 minutes. Select "MATCH" followed by the "START / STOP" button.
5. When zone 1 time reaches 10 minutes, turn the fritters over; cook them for a further 10 minutes, until thoroughly cooked.
Bon appétit!

MEDITERRANEAN VEGAN SAUSAGE

Serves 6
Prep time: 10 minutes
Cook time: 20 minutes

Per Serving:
Calories: 268
Fat: 6.6g
Carbs: 39.4g
Fiber: 10.3g
Protein: 14.4g

- 400g can red kidney beans, drained • 400g can butter beans, drained
- 1 tbsp olive oil • 1 tbsp sunflower seeds
- 2 tbsp flaxseed meal • 4 garlic cloves, peeled
- 1 medium onion, peeled and quartered
- 1 tbsp walnut halves
- 50g oat flour
- 1 tsp baking powder
- 1 tbsp Mediterranean herb mix
- 1 tsp ground cumin
- Sea salt and freshly ground black pepper, to taste

1. Insert crisper plates in both drawers. Spray crisper plates with nonstick cooking oil.
2. In your blender or food processor, blend all the ingredients until everything is well incorporated.
3. Form the mixture into a sausage shape and place the sausages in the cooking basket.
4. Select zone 1 and pair it with "AIR FRY" at 180°C for 20 minutes. Select "MATCH" followed by the "START / STOP" button.
5. When zone 1 time reaches 10 minutes, turn the sausages over using silicone-tipped tongs.
6. Reinsert the drawers to continue cooking. Bon appétit!

BAKED BEANS WITH MARINATED BASIL TOFU

Serves 6
Prep time: 10 minutes
Cook time: 20 minutes

Per Serving:
Calories: 386
Fat: 16.6g
Carbs: 39.3g
Fiber: 15.6g
Protein: 25.4g

- 300g dry cannellini beans, soaked overnight
- 1 rosemary sprig • 1 bay leaf
- 1 tbsp olive oil
- 400g tofu, cubed
- 2 tbsp basil leaves, chopped
- 2 tbsp marinara sauce
- 2 large garlic cloves, thinly sliced
- 1 large onion, sliced
- 200ml chicken stock

1. Add the beans, rosemary, and bay leaf to a large pan; add enough water to cover them by 3-4 cm. Bring to a rapid boil and immediately turn the heat to a simmer. Let the beans simmer for about 30 minutes until they're tender.
2. In the meantime, marinate the tofu with basil, marinara, and garlic.
3. Transfer the beans to two lightly greased baking trays; add the other ingredients, including the marinated tofu, and stir to combine. Add the trays to the cooking basket.
4. Select zone 1 and pair it with "BAKE" at 180°C for 20 minutes. Select "MATCH" followed by the "START / STOP" button.
5. Serve with your favourite Mediterranean salad, if desired. Devour!

Serves 6
Prep time: 10 minutes
Cook time: 12 minutes

Per Serving:
Calories: 288
Fat: 12.6g
Carbs: 32.8g
Fiber: 6.4g
Protein: 15.5g

- 3 medium courgettes, halved lengthways
Stuffing:
- 400g Italian brown mushrooms, chopped
- 200g canned red lentils, drained and rinsed
- 2 garlic cloves, minced
- 1 large red onion, chopped
- 2 tbsp Italian parsley, chopped
- 4 tbsp marinara sauce
- Sea salt and cracked black pepper, to taste
Sauce:
- 60g pine nuts
- 2 tbsp olive oil
- 1 tbsp fresh lemon juice
- 2 tbsp nutritional yeast (vegan parmesan)

1. Pat the courgette dry with kitchen towels.
2. In a bowl, mix the ingredients for the stuffing; mix until everything is well incorporated. Divide the stuffing mixture between the prepared courgette halves.
3. Lower the stuffed courgettes into both drawers.
4. Meanwhile, blend all the sauce ingredients until creamy and smooth.
5. Select zone 1 and pair it with "AIR FRY" at 190°C for 12 minutes. Select "MATCH" followed by the "START / STOP" button.
6. When zone 1 time reaches 6 minutes, top them with the nutty "cheesy" sauce and continue to cook for a further 6 minutes, until cooked through.

CHAPTER 8
DESSERTS

MEDITERRANEAN FLAPJACKS

Serves 8
Prep time: 10 minutes
Cook time: 15 minutes

Per Serving:
Calories: 227
Fat: 4.9g
Carbs: 36.8g
Fiber: 2.2g
Protein: 7.7g

- 1 tbsp butter, melted
- 2 eggs, beaten
- 100ml almond milk
- 1 tsp vanilla extract
- 1 / 2 tsp anise, ground
- 250g plain flour
- 150g oat flour
- A pinch of kosher salt
- A pinch of ground cinnamon

1. Grease 8 muffin cases with butter and set them aside.
2. Beat the eggs with almond milk, vanilla and anise until pale and frothy. Gradually stir in the other dry ingredients; beat the mixture with an electric mixer to ensure no lumps are created.
3. Divide the batter between the prepared muffin cases.
4. Select zone 1 and pair it with "BAKE" at 180°C for 15 minutes. Select "MATCH" followed by the "START / STOP" button.

Bon appétit!

MEDITERRANEAN FRUIT CRISP

Serves 7
Prep time: 10 minutes
Cook time: 30 minutes

Per Serving:
Calories: 227
Fat: 4.9g
Carbs: 36.8g
Fiber: 2.2g
Protein: 7.7g

- 2 tsp butter, room temperature
- 2 medium figs, sliced
- 60g golden caster sugar
- 1 / 2 tsp ground cardamom
- A pinch of grated nutmeg
- Topping:
- 100g quick-cooking oats
- 40ml coconut oil, melted
- 100g pistachios, chopped
- 100g brown sugar
- 1 tsp vanilla extract
- 3 medium peaches, stoned and sliced
- 1 tbsp rum
- 2 tbsp cornstarch
- 1 / 2 tsp ground cinnamon

1. Grease two baking trays with butter and set them aside.
2. Toss your fruits with rum, golden caster sugar, cornstarch, and spices. Arrange the fruits in the prepared trays.
3. In a bowl, thoroughly combine all the topping ingredients until a crumb-like texture has formed. Scatter the topping mixture all over the fruit.
4. Lower the baking trays into the cooking basket.
5. Select zone 1 and pair it with "BAKE" at 165°C for 30 minutes. Select "MATCH" followed by the "START / STOP" button.

Devour!

TAHINI ALMOND COOKIES

Serves 8
Prep time: 15 minutes
Cook time: 15 minutes

Per Serving:
Calories: 282
Fat: 16.4g
Carbs: 28.5g
Fiber: 3.9g
Protein: 8.1g

- 100g plain flour
- 1 tsp baking powder
- 100g almond flour
- 120g golden syrup
- 1 large egg, beaten, room temperature
- 60g tahini, chilled
- 1 tsp vanilla extract
- 1 / 2 tsp ground cinnamon
- 120ml almond milk
- 80g almonds, chopped

1. Begin by preheating your Air Fryer to 180°C for 5 minutes.
2. In a mixing bowl, thoroughly combine the dry ingredients; mix until your mixture resembles breadcrumbs.
3. In another bowl, thoroughly combine all the liquid ingredients. Add the wet mixture to the dry ingredients; fold in the chopped almonds and stir to combine well.
4. Shape the balls using an ice cream scoop, and then, arrange them on the parchment-lined baking tins.
5. Select zone 1 and pair it with "BAKE" at 180°C for 15 minutes. Select "MATCH" followed by the "START / STOP" button.
6. Let your cookies sit on a cooling rack for about 10 minutes before serving. Devour!

CLASSIC MUG CAKE

Serves 4
Prep time: 10 minutes
Cook time: 10 minutes

Per Serving:
Calories: 386
Fat: 17.4g
Carbs: 50.5g
Fiber: 3.9g
Protein: 9.1g

- 2 large bananas, peeled and mashed
- 4 medium eggs
- 2 tbsp coconut oil
- A pinch of ground cinnamon
- 1 tsp vanilla extract
- 100ml Mediterranean honey
- 50g oat flour
- 1 tsp baking powder
- 50g chocolate chips

1. Beat the eggs until pale and frothy; add the other ingredients and mix to combine well.
2. Divide the ingredients between four ramekins. Lower the ramekins into both drawers.
3. Select zone 1 and pair it with "BAKE" at 180°C for 10 minutes. Select "MATCH" followed by the "START / STOP" button.
Devour!

CHOCOLATE PISTACHIO SQUARES

Serves 9
Prep time: 10 minutes
Cook time: 15 minutes

Per Serving:
Calories: 436
Fat: 26.4g
Carbs: 43.1g
Fiber: 6.2g
Protein: 10.1g

- 200g porridge oats
- 100g Sultanas
- 60g sunflower seed
- 60g pumpkin seeds
- 80g coconut oil, room temperature
- 100g clear Mediterranean honey
- 100g dark chocolate chunks
- 100g pistachios, chopped

1. Begin by preheating your Ninja Dual Zone Air Fryer to 180°C for 5 minutes.
2. In a mixing bowl, thoroughly combine all ingredients.
3. Spoon the mixture into two parchment-lined roasting tins, pressing down with a wide spatula. Lower the tins into the cooking basket.
4. Select zone 1 and pair it with "BAKE" at 180°C for 15 minutes. Select "MATCH" followed by the "START / STOP" button.
5. Let it cool before slicing it into bars. Enjoy!

TRADITIONAL OLIVE OIL BROWNIES

Serves 9
Prep time: 10 minutes
Cook time: 20 minutes

Per Serving:
Calories: 246
Fat: 9.4g
Carbs: 40g
Fiber: 3.2g
Protein: 7.8g

- 100g olive oil
- 100ml Greek yoghurt
- 150g golden caster sugar
- 2 medium eggs, lightly beaten
- 100g oat flour
- 100g almond flour
- 80g cocoa powder
- 1 tsp ground cinnamon
- 1 tsp pure vanilla paste

1. Grease two baking tins with cooking oil.
2. Beat the eggs until pale and frothy. Stir in the other ingredients and mix until everything is well combined.
3. Select zone 1 and pair it with "BAKE" at 170°C for 20 minutes. Select "MATCH" followed by the "START / STOP" button.
4. Allow your brownies to rest on a cooling rack for about 10 minutes before cutting and serving. Devour!

APPLE AND ALMOND FRITTERS

Serves 6
Prep time: 10 minutes
Cook time: 18 minutes

Per Serving:
Calories: 313
Fat: 11.4g
Carbs: 46.2g
Fiber: 3.6g
Protein: 7.7g

- 200g self-raising flour
- 1 tsp vanilla extract
- A pinch of sea salt
- 2 eggs
- 60g golden caster sugar
- 100ml almond milk
- 2 medium apples, cored and grated
- 50g almonds, chopped
- 2 tbsp olive oil
- 1 / 2 tsp baking powder
- 1 tsp cinnamon powder

1. Line both drawers with parchment paper.
2. In a mixing bowl, thoroughly combine the dry ingredients.
3. Then, separate the egg yolk from the egg white. Beat the egg yolk with the sugar and milk. Beat the egg white until stiff peaks form.
4. Gradually add the egg white to the egg yolk mixture.
5. Add the liquid ingredients to the dry ingredients; fold in the grated apples and almonds; stir to combine well.
6. Use a cookie scoop to create the dollops of batter and arrange them in both drawers. Drizzle your fritters with olive oil.
7. Select zone 1 and pair it with "AIR FRY" at 180°C for 18 minutes. Select "MATCH" followed by the "START / STOP" button.

Bon appétit!

CINNAMON FIG CRUMBLE

Serves 8
Prep time: 10 minutes
Cook time: 30 minutes

Per Serving:
Calories: 347
Fat: 13.4g
Carbs: 54.4g
Fiber: 5g
Protein: 5.7g

- 2 tsp coconut oil, room temperature
- 2 tbsp cornstarch
- 1 tsp ground cardamom
Topping:
- 100g quick-cooking oats
- 100g almonds, finely chopped
- 100g brown sugar
- 1 tsp vanilla extract
- 9 medium figs, sliced
- 60g golden caster sugar
- A pinch of grated nutmeg
- 40ml coconut oil, melted
- 4 tbsp Sultanas

1. Grease two baking trays with 2 teaspoons of coconut oil; set them aside.
2. Toss your figs with the cornstarch, sugar, and spices. Arrange the figs in the prepared trays.
3. In a bowl, thoroughly combine all the topping ingredients until a crumb-like texture has formed. Scatter the topping mixture all over the figs.
4. Lower the baking trays into the cooking basket.
5. Select zone 1 and pair it with "BAKE" at 165°C for 30 minutes. Select "MATCH" followed by the "START / STOP" button. Devour!

CRUNCHY APPLE RINGS

Serves 2
Prep time: 10 minutes
Cook time: 18 minutes

Per Serving:
Calories: 247
Fat: 11.4g
Carbs: 38.4g
Fiber: 5g
Protein: 4.5g

- 1 large apple, cored and sliced
- 2 tbsp tahini
- A pinch of ground cinnamon
- A pinch of grated nutmeg
- 2 tbsp clear honey
- 2 tbsp pistachios, chopped

1. Toss apple slices with tahini, cinnamon, nutmeg, and honey. Then, place them in the foil-lined cooking basket.
2. Select zone 1 and pair it with "ROAST" at 185°C for 18 minutes. Select "MATCH" followed by the "START / STOP" button.
3. When zone 1 time reaches 10 minutes, add pistachios, and reinsert the drawers to continue cooking.

Bon appétit!

LEMON COOKIES WITH PISTACHIO (KOULARAKIA)

Serves 8
Prep time: 10 minutes
Cook time: 15 minutes

Per Serving:
Calories: 362
Fat: 25.5g
Carbs: 27.5g
Fiber: 6g
Protein: 10.1g

- 250g almond flour
- 150g golden syrup
- 60g tahini, chilled
- 1 / 2 tsp cardamom, ground
- 1 / 2 tsp ground cinnamon
- 120ml almond milk
- 100g pistachios, chopped
- 1 tsp baking powder
- 1 tbsp lemon juice, freshly squeezed
- 1 tsp vanilla extract

1. Start by preheating your Air Fryer to 180°C for 5 minutes.
2. In a mixing bowl, thoroughly combine the dry ingredients. In another bowl, thoroughly combine all the liquid ingredients.
3. Add the wet mixture to the dry ingredients; fold in the chopped pistachios and stir to combine well.
4. Roll the chilled dough into strips. (You can twist them to make twisted rope shapes). Now, arrange your cookies on the parchment-lined baking tins.
5. Select zone 1 and pair it with "BAKE" at 180°C for 15 minutes. Select "MATCH" followed by the "START / STOP" button.
6. Let your cookies sit on a cooling rack for about 10 minutes before serving. Devour!

INDEX

Printed by Amazon Italia Logistica S.r.l.
Torrazza Piemonte (TO), Italy

57564658R00047